THE
BALLOT
BOX

THE BALLOT BOX

10 Presidential Elections That Changed American History

Chris Barsanti

FALL RIVER PRESS

New York

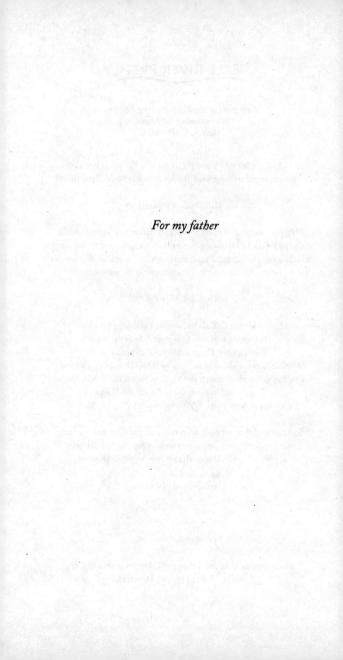

For my father

FALL RIVER PRESS

New York

An Imprint of Sterling Publishing Co., Inc.
1166 Avenue of the Americas
New York, NY 10036

ISBN 978-1-4351-7062-9

Distributed in Canada by Sterling Publishing Co., Inc.
c/o Canadian Manda Group, 664 Annette Street
Toronto, Ontario M6S 2C8, Canada
Distributed in the United Kingdom by GMC Distribution Services
Castle Place, 166 High Street, Lewes, East Sussex BN7 1XU, England
Distributed in Australia by NewSouth Books
University of New South Wales, Sydney, NSW 2052, Australia

For information about custom editions, special sales, and premium
and corporate purchases, please contact Sterling Special Sales
at 800-805-5489 or specialsales@sterlingpublishing.com.

Manufactured in Canada

2 4 6 8 10 9 7 5 3 1

sterlingpublishing.com

Image credits: Courtesy **Library of Congress:** endpapers, xii,
16, 54, 70, 88, 146, 187; **Dover:** viii

CONTENTS

INTRODUCTION

A REPUBLIC, IF YOU CAN KEEP IT...

Presidents, especially in the modern era, have incredible powers. Wielding broad discretionary authorities, they can dispatch military forces around the globe, send emergency funding to a disaster zone, veto Congressional legislation, make treaties, nominate Supreme Court justices for lifetime appointments, select a large cadre of diplomats and senior officials to carry out their bidding around the country and the world, pardon those convicted of crimes, and if they so desire, launch nuclear weapons at any time of the day or night.

At the same time, the office of the president comes with significant weaknesses. Nearly every power of the executive branch enumerated above is constrained to some degree by one or both of the other two branches of government: Congress and the judiciary. Vetoes can be overridden, judges and cabinet members can fail to be confirmed, extended military deployments can be challenged or defunded, and the president's time in office can potentially be curtailed by an impeachment trial.

The president is ultimately a powerful but deeply constrained executive. This is how the Founding Fathers imagined it. Their chief fears for the new republic were tyranny from below and tyranny from above. The first fear, as you will read later, was managed by checks on the ability of majority votes to override the desires of a minority. The second was dealt with by the restrictions placed on a president, particularly their limited time in office. Every four years, another group of candidates make their arguments to the American people about why they are the best choice for leadership. It is an imperfect system, subject to everything from disinformation to vote tampering, which does not consistently produce meritocratic excellence. But the flex and give built into the governmental framework generally allows for enough balance that the more effective leaders tend to get rewarded at the ballot box while the most ineffective or even criminal ones get shunted out either through impeachment or, more commonly, through losing reelection. Usually.

Each presidential election, then, is a chance for the country not only to judge the leadership qualities of a potential new head of state but also to take part in a referendum on what Americans find important. In one election, a majority of voters might want a president who seems able to fix a troubled economy. In another, they could veer toward a strong military leader. Not infrequently, voting decisions can also be based on factors such as personality or smart campaigning that have little to do with the job at hand.

Each time, though, the ultimate decision plays a significant role in determining what direction the country will be heading in over the next four years. That is why voters are so often told that the upcoming election is the most important one of their lifetimes. While that cliché has been shamelessly overused by pundits and operatives to hype a candidate or boost turnout over the years, there are times when it is actually somewhat true.

Some elections happen at hinge moments in American history, when titanic debates over everything from slavery to war to a government's moral duty to address poverty hang in the balance. Especially in those years, a vote for a Republican, a Democrat, a Whig, or a Populist signals not only support for a particular candidate but also a statement of belief in what kind of country America should be. The ten presidential elections you will read about in this book occurred when the American democratic experiment was being critically reexamined and reshaped by millions of citizens.

That continual flux of democracy is a large part of its strength, allowing for changes that can tackle issues not conceived of or addressed at the founding. The continual shifts from one political party to another can also be a weakness, sometimes creating a whiplash effect. This chaotic and fraught dynamism is part of what Ben Franklin meant when he was asked at the end of the Constitutional Convention in 1787: ". . . what have we got—a republic or a monarchy?" and he replied, "A republic, if you can keep it."

These ten elections each represent large gambles on the future of the republic and often radically divergent beliefs about what is required to keep it intact for the future.

JOHN ADAMS
VS.
THOMAS JEFFERSON

It is difficult now to avoid the "golden age" fallacy in thinking of the era of the Founders. . . . [To] the first presidents as well as to their critics, the early years of the republic probably seemed more like a time of troubles than a golden age.[1]

—C. Vann Woodward

Our Obligations to our Country never cease but with our Lives.

—John Adams

★ ★ ★ ★ ★ ★ ★

—— **The Candidates** ——

*President: John Adams
Party: Federalist
Electoral Votes: 71

Vice President: Thomas Jefferson
Party: Democratic-Republicans
Electoral Votes: 68

* = Winning candidates

WHY IT MATTERED

The election of 1796 might seem like a strange place to begin this journey. It could be argued that the first election, in 1789, was the most consequential that America ever faced. In that year, the United States of America was not even a nation yet, but rather an idea only vaguely understood by the four million or so ex-British subjects scattered along the Eastern seaboard. It took some trial and error for that idea to get worked out. The first two presidential elections in 1789 and 1792, which featured neither political parties nor a popular vote, could be seen as practice runs for the real thing.

Three years after the Treaty of Paris officially concluded the Revolutionary War, the fledgling American experiment faced its own uprising. Shays' Rebellion (1786–1787) was just a small, quickly defeated insurrection over taxation and debtor relief, but it helped convince the Continental Congress of the need for a more robust central government than the one allowed by the governing Articles of Confederation.

During the summer of 1787, at the Constitutional Convention in Philadelphia, a political structure emerged. The new Constitution's elegant tripartite framework of executive, legislative, and judicial branches, each checking and balancing the other, was hammered out over the next two years.

In later years, historians would marvel at America's fortune. Most revolutionary governments saw their leadership tear itself apart in power struggles before settling into illiberal structures resembling the regimes they had overthrown. Setting America apart was a leadership composed of highly literate students of the Enlightenment, who were nearly as concerned about avoiding the dark side of popular rule as they were about holding monarchism at bay. Because of that concern, even though the writers of the Constitution wanted a popular vote and a president, they built in firebreaks to distribute governing powers and to keep mob rule or a tyrant from overwhelming the system.

Pro-centralized government advocates like Alexander Hamilton and James Madison penned the essays that became *The Federalist Papers*. Meanwhile, anti-Federalists like Patrick Henry pushed for more local powers and the inclusion of the Bill of Rights. The Constitution was ratified by enough states to take effect in 1788. The first presidential election was held in February 1789, six years after the defeat of the British Empire in the Revolutionary War.

That first election was very close to a coronation. Given the revered status of Revolutionary War hero George Washington, his selection as the nation's first leader was a given. While reserved as always and extremely reluctant to accept the mantle, he knew there was nobody else for the job. In fact, delegates at the Constitutional Convention essentially designed the position with him in mind. There would be no popular vote. In *Federalist 68*, Hamilton argued that the populace's "heats and ferments" would be tempered by electors selected "from the general mass." The president was determined by the Electoral College, which remains the true determinant of an election's winner.

On February 4, 1789, sixty-nine electors—selected by popular vote or by their state legislature—gathered in New York City, the nation's first capital, to elect a president. They all voted for Washington. John Adams was elected as vice president. (At the time, vice presidents were not selected by presidential candidates. They were elected separately.)

Washington led the nascent government as he did colonial irregulars in the French and Indian War and the entire Revolutionary Army: with great care and a mania for detail that somehow never kept him from taking bold, dramatic action. He knew that as the first president, almost everything he did mattered. "I walk on untrodden ground," he wrote in 1790. "There is scarcely any part of my conduct which may not hereafter be drawn into precedent." Washington's regular conferences with his four executive secretaries started the tradition of each president having a cabinet, a practice which is mentioned nowhere in the Constitution.

In 1792, Washington was unanimously reelected, with Adams again squeaking through as vice president. In the intervening years, a more revenge-minded revolution had bloodily swept away the French monarchy, Secretary of the Treasury Hamilton began erecting the institutional scaffolding of a modern federal state, and the seeds of political parties (a development feared by the drafters of the Constitution) took root.

The unifying popularity of Washington helped carry the former colonies through a period of vulnerability, and his intense commitment to democracy ensured that the new republic did not fall prey to the temptations of a strongman leader.

Nevertheless, Washington soon tired of criticism from opinionated journalists. "[I]f the Government and the officers of it are to be the constant theme for News-paper abuse," he wrote in a gloomy letter to Edmund Randolph, whom he had appointed as America's first Attorney General, "it will be impossible, I conceive, for any man living to manage the helm or to keep the machine together." He decided not to run for a third term, setting a tradition that held until the twentieth century.

In 1796, the real work of building America would begin.

KING GEORGE

—∞∞∞—

Washington may not have actually been offered the chance to be a king rather than a democratically selected president, as the story is sometimes told. But according to historian Ron Chernow, the pomp and circumstance of Washington's selection were certainly royal in character. His journey from Mount Vernon to New York for the election was akin to a "royal procession," filled with "ceremonial distractions" and "festivities" that discomfited the soon-to-be president, who was uncomfortable being the center of attention on the best of days. Chernow wrote that after the oath of office was administered in Federal Hall in lower Manhattan, the people bellowed "Long live our beloved president" as though, according to Chernow, they were signaling support for the monarchy and shouting "Long live the king!"[2]

JOHN ADAMS

America was due for some whiplash in 1796. The onetime colony had only recently absorbed the cognitive dissonance of having a democratic leader rather than a monarch. Then, within a few short years, they had to wrap their heads around the idea that they would be led by someone other than Washington. Massachusetts Congressman Fisher Ames termed the transfer of power to a mere mortal a "transmigration."[3] Though there was not exactly a surfeit of tall, imposing, Roman statesman-like war heroes with sterling reputations like Washington's to go around in America, the first choices the nation would face could hardly have been more different.

Witty, moody, and often unpleasant but inarguably brilliant, John Adams was a Massachusetts Puritan and Harvard-educated lawyer of shaky health who never served a day in uniform. He became involved in the American independence cause after protests against the 1765 Stamp Act, lending his prodigious and restless intellect to writing propaganda and newspaper columns.

In an inauspicious start for a future president that showed his contrarian and idealist streaks, he gained popular notice in 1770, when he took the job of defending the British soldiers accused of killing five protestors in the Boston Massacre. "Facts are stubborn things," he famously argued to the jury, attempting to cool down anti-Crown passions through the classic defense-lawyer strategy of appealing to high-minded fairness while also impugning the alleged victims, in this case terming them a "motley rabble." All but two defendants were declared innocent and none went to prison.

Showing an early ability to leap into controversy and survive, Adams built a profile in the federation of like-minded thinkers and rebels agitating for American independence. A delegate to the first two Continental Congresses, he served on a staggering number of committees. In 1775, he nominated Washington to command the Continental Army. In 1776, he dashed off the pamphlet "Thoughts on Government," arguing that "A single assembly is liable to all the vices, follies, and frailties of an individual"[4] and sketching out a three-pillar government structure (executive, legislative, judicial), which he thought could save a future democratic America from a too-powerful executive or mob rule. He also built a career as a diplomat, helping to negotiate the end of the Revolutionary War and serving as the first "United States Minister Plenipotentiary to the Court of St. James" (i.e., ambassador to England).

After returning to America, Adams was twice elected vice president to George Washington. During his time in office, Adams ultimately threw in with the Federalist faction even though he had misgivings about overly centralized power and openly despised the idea of political parties. Frustrated by the vice presidency's lack of power, by 1796, Adams was ready for the real thing.

THOMAS JEFFERSON

The dual-party system was in place by the time of America's first contested election. Founded in 1791, the Federalists had consolidated power in Washington's administration. Rising in reaction to the Federalists (urban, Northern, centralized-government oriented, distrustful of too much democracy) were the Democratic-Republicans (rural, Southern, states'-rights oriented, suspicious of top-down authority), led by Revolutionary leaders like Thomas Jefferson.

Unlike Adams, the stout and retiring New Englander, Jefferson was a tall, robust, redheaded outdoorsman and Virginian gentleman farmer. Like Adams, he was an eloquent lawyer and part of the brain trust that crafted the nation's founding documents. Jefferson embodied the contradictions of many Founding Fathers. Despite authoring most of the Declaration of Independence (one early draft included a section excoriating King George III for trafficking slaves), he owned many enslaved people, including one, Sally Hemings, who was his mistress. A purported champion of the small farmer, he operated a large plantation. A proud populist, he was also an Enlightenment intellectual with a knack for classical languages. He was resolutely not self-contradictory on the issue of the division between church and state—one of the main themes of his short 1785 treatise on democracy and freedom, *Notes on the State of Virginia*.

After stints as governor of Virginia and ambassador to France, Jefferson served as Secretary of State to Washington. He resigned in 1793 in opposition to Hamilton's creation of the federal Treasury. While further disturbed by Federalist innovations like the excise tax—which he blamed for the "Whiskey Rebellion" of 1794—Jefferson still wanted to stay out of electoral politics. Nevertheless, Federalism, which insisted on centralized power, seemed to him an insult to democracy and enticed him into the arena.

THE ELECTION

Many elections have dramatic consequences. But the lines in 1796 could hardly have been drawn more starkly. Not only would the election help determine the course of the nation while it was still forming and testing its new governing institutions, but it would also need to prove that despite growing polarization, America would not descend into the kind of factional violence that had destroyed other republics.

Of the two leading factions, the Federalists appeared to have the upper hand going into the election, given that two of their leading lights (Hamilton and Madison) had been key members of Washington's administration. But there was growing support for the Democratic-Republicans, fed by enthusiasm for the raw fervor of the French Revolution and a distrust of the growing class of bankers and traders.

Despite tensions between the factions—supercharged by rancor over the Federalist-backed Jay's Treaty with Britain in 1794, which seemed to many Democratic-Republicans to mean far too much entanglement with Europe—there was no open electoral contest for most of the year. The political establishment assumed Washington was not running for a third term. It was common knowledge that Adams and Jefferson both wanted the office next, but neither seemed able to admit it.

Further complicating matters, Washington was coy about his intentions. He finally announced he would not seek a third term in September. This did not leave much time for campaigning. *Not* that candidates were supposed to campaign. During that more decorous time, it was not considered appropriate for candidates to haul around the country kissing babies and delivering stump speeches. While ideological rivals, Adams and Jefferson remained friends and ". . . refused to bloody their noses in partisan warfare."[5] By the end of the year, Jefferson was still acting as though he had no intention of being president, claiming in a letter to Adams that "I have no ambition to govern men. It is a painful and thankless office."[6]

The true election was waged by subordinates via newspapers and arm-twisting of the electors who were selected starting in November. Consistently seen as the front-runner, Adams prevailed in February 1797 with 71 votes. Coming in second with 68, Jefferson was named vice president. Ironically, as the sitting vice president, Adams was also head of the Senate and so responsible for counting ballots and declaring his own victory. In a further twist, Jefferson owed his second-place win to an adversary. Some behind-the-scenes wrangling by Hamilton to divert votes from his rival Adams backfired, which resulted in more electors voting for Jefferson.

THE AFTERMATH

The results of the 1796 election were polarizing in a way familiar to modern readers, with the North going mostly for Adams and the South supporting Jefferson. Another similarity could be found in the South's distorted representation. In a surreal compromise, the drafters of the Constitution had allowed slave-owning states to count each slave as three-fifths of a person when determining the number of their representatives. This allowed slave states to gain inflated power at the expense of people without rights, much as they continued to do post-Emancipation, through voter suppression. Despite a demonstrably imperfect process, however, the 1796 election showed that America could achieve a transfer of power without resorting to violence or monarchical succession.

As the first and only Federalist presidential victory, 1796 also presaged great changes. At first, Adams and Jefferson's friendship and dedication to the American democratic experiment helped paper over their (and the country's) sharp ideological differences. But reality quickly intervened.

When Adams was sworn in on March 4, 1797, the country was in an uproar over the seizure of hundreds of American merchant ships by the French. Diplomatic entreaties were met by the French with a demand for a bribe, a loan, and an apology from American diplomats. Once this became public knowledge, the XYZ Affair (so-called because the names of the French envoys were kept secret) exacerbated the acrimony raging between pro-British Federalists and pro-French Democratic-Republicans. Fueled by a swiftly expanding and viciously partisan press, the debate occasionally broke out into mob violence.

To tamp down dissent, the Federalist-controlled Congress passed the infamous Alien and Sedition Acts. Among other things, the Acts gave the president sweeping powers of deportation and censorship. Even though the Acts expired or were repealed within a few years, it was not before several journalists, including Ben Franklin's grandson, were thrown in jail. These harsh authoritarian measures and deep unpopularity left a stain on the presidency of Adams. He tried to blame Hamilton, though the Acts passed with his tacit support.[7]

Much of Adams' presidency was taken up with crises around the prospect of war with France, with deep enmity between the pro- and anti-camps. This reflected poorly on the president, whose administration was termed a "reign of witches" by the stewing vice president. Despite it all, the ever-prickly Adams remained proud that he kept the so-called "Quasi-War" with France from turning into a real war.

Following a determined smear campaign against Adams—one pamphlet called him a "hideous hermaphroditical character"—and the continued anti-Adams campaigning by the fiercely pro-war Hamilton, the divided Federalists entered the 1800 election in weakened shape. Democratic-Republicans ran Jefferson and Aaron Burr, who were opposed by Federalist candidates Adams and Charles C. Pinckney. (Parties did not then nominate candidates for specific roles; whoever garnered the most votes became president, and the runner-up was made vice president.) After several days, dozens of tied votes in the House, and heated rhetoric about the will of the people, Jefferson was declared the winner.

Jefferson was sworn into office in March 1801, five months after Adams had moved into the damp and unfinished first presidential residence in the new capital of Washington, D.C. "May none but Honest and Wise Men ever rule under This Roof," Adams wrote to Abigail, a high-reaching wish carved into the White House's State Dining Room mantel in 1945.

CALLENDER, THE HIRED GUN

—◇◇◇◇◇—

A one-man character assassination squad, the Scottish-born James Callender was the most infamous hired hack in post–Revolutionary War America. A fervent partisan journalist, he was one of the few writers who dared criticize Washington (calling him "debauched"). Despite an outward preference for decorum, Jefferson backed Callender financially, likely approving of attacks such as the campaign to smear Adams as a warmonger and the 1797 pamphlet that publicized Alexander Hamilton's affair with a married woman. After being fined and briefly jailed under the Sedition Act, Callender requested a sinecure from Jefferson: postmaster of Richmond, Virginia. Jefferson balked, worried that the hatchet man posed a risk. In revenge, Callender published a 1802 article claiming that Jefferson had fathered a son with one of his slaves: "Her name is SALLY." Like many yellow journalists consumed by their own bile, Callender's life unraveled quickly. He died in 1803, drowning in the James River while most likely drunk.

WHAT IF...?

Jefferson claimed relief at his 1796 loss, as the new president would have the "shadow of Washington"[8] looming over him. Given that Washington's shadow was still notably long when Jefferson took over the office four years later, this statement should be taken with a few grains of salt.

Ultimately, the 1796 election was crucial to the formation of America due to its enshrinement of a peaceful transfer of power. Despite their many differences in background and ideology, Jefferson and Adams were in many ways quite alike in temperament. Many might guess that a decentralized government advocate like Jefferson would never have pushed for a standing navy like Adams did. But the ardent anti-Federalist (and theoretical pacifist) ultimately expanded the role of government. Jefferson launched America's first foreign intervention by sending the Navy in 1804 to assault the Tripoli base of the Barbary pirates who had declared war after America ended the long tradition of paying tribute to keep its ships safe. Jefferson also doubled the nation's size with the Louisiana Purchase, a land grab that the president went ahead with even though he worried it was unconstitutional. After all, at about four cents an acre, it was a great deal.

If Jefferson had won the presidency in 1796, chances are that he would have navigated most of the day's major issues in a fashion similar to Adams. He would, however, most likely not have pushed for the Alien and Sedition Acts. Under his rule, the already weakened Federalists would have come to an even earlier end. With the more unified Democratic-Republican party behind him, Jefferson almost certainly would have been more popular than the disputatious Adams, and it's possible he would have become the first president to serve three terms.

★ ★ ★ **1828** ★ ★ ★

ANDREW JACKSON
– vs. –
JOHN QUINCY ADAMS

General Jackson is hated by the aristocracy, and termed an usurper and a despot, a cutthroat and a villain.

—William Leggett

Do they think that I am such a damned fool as to think myself fit for President of the United States?

—Andrew Jackson

★ ★ ★ ★ ★ ★ ★

— The Candidates —

*President: Andrew Jackson
*Vice President: John C. Calhoun
Party: Democratic
Popular / Electoral Votes: 647,286 / 178

President: John Quincy Adams
Vice President: Richard Rush
Party: National Republican
Popular / Electoral Votes: 508,064 / 83

* = Winning candidates

WHY IT MATTERED

In America's first few decades, when the fledgling nation was finding its legs, the rumblings of war from across the Atlantic were a continual distraction. Jefferson was one of America's most committed visionaries of individual freedoms, but he had limited success aligning the government to those ends. Barely squeaking into office in 1800 and resoundingly reelected in 1804, his presidency was dominated by foreign affairs, excepting the massive westward expansion of the Louisiana Purchase.

By the time he left office (respecting the unwritten two-term precedent established by Washington), the embargo he had imposed on Great Britain and France as punishment for disrupting American trade was wreaking havoc on the domestic economy. Following Jefferson as president was James Madison, a key architect of the Constitution. During his presidency, Congress declared war against Great Britain in June of 1812.

But the end of the Napoleonic Wars in 1815 brought a general reduction in international tensions. This allowed the country to turn its gaze inward for a brief period that Boston's *Columbian Centinel* newspaper termed the "Era of Good Feelings." It was propitious timing for an isolationist shift. The population had grown from 5.3 million in 1800 to 9.6 million in 1820. At the same time, the Louisiana Purchase opened vast tracts of land for new settlement, following the violent expulsion of Indian tribes.

James Monroe, the third Virginian Democratic-Republican in a row to serve two terms as president (1817–1825), articulated the nation's mood with his 1823 annual message to Congress. He declared that the Western Hemisphere was henceforth an American sphere of influence. European powers were to halt further expansions. Little noticed at the time, the so-called "Monroe Doctrine," written by Monroe's Secretary of State John Quincy Adams, was one of America's first stirrings as an imperial power.

Furthering the impression of domestic unity was the reality of something near one-party rule. During Jefferson, Madison, Monroe, and John Quincy Adams's (1825–1829) twenty-eight years in office, Democratic-Republicans held not only the presidency but also both houses of Congress. The judiciary was the only hold-out of increasingly isolated Federalists, many of whom had been appointed by John Adams on his way out (the so-called "midnight judges").

But the era's end was signaled in the 1820s by growing dissatisfaction from multiple directions. Northern states, having outlawed slavery and seeing greater immigration, were building complex economies marked more by manufacturing and trade than farming. By contrast, the South remained firmly in the economic and political status quo, its fortunes tied to "King Cotton," a monocrop slave labor economy that gilded its base cruelty with an aristocratic patina. Regional divisions grew heated as states were added through westward expansion, each one setting off a new controversy over whether it would allow slavery, thereby potentially upending the delicate North-South balance.

Another issue that tied together several vectors of angst was concern over the seeming disconnection between elections and their results. This was highlighted in the election of 1824, the first to count the popular vote for the presidency. With no Federalists of note remaining, the field was crowded with candidates from the increasingly splintered Democratic-Republicans.

The three-way tie between John Quincy Adams, Tennessee senator Andrew Jackson, and Secretary of the Treasury William Crawford was decided in favor of Adams by the House of Representatives. To many, this highlighted the ugly reality that ultimately the contest would be decided by the same clique of politicians.[1] Reacting to the rumor that Adams secured his victory by promising House Speaker Henry Clay—one of the "war hawks" in the House who pushed to launch hostilities with Great Britain in 1812—the position of Secretary of State, Jackson termed the election the "corrupt bargain."

Hoping to highlight his incorruptibility, Adams kept on pro-Jackson partisans and avoided nominating party loyalists for federal posts. But he gained no traction. Clay worried that Adams "intended to neglect or abandon his friends in order to woo his enemies."[2] A misunderstanding of popular sentiment, in addition to an inability to pass meaningful legislation, plagued Adams through his term and may have left him blind to the coming tidal wave.

ANDREW JACKSON

Andrew Jackson was not the first true fighting man to be president. George Washington had seen his share of brutal hand-to-hand combat. But Jackson was the only president to have fought in both the American Revolution and the War of 1812. He was also, so far as we know, the only man to take the oath of office with a bullet lodged in his chest.

Jackson grew up further from privilege than the presidents who preceded him. Born in 1767 and raised a devout Presbyterian in the Carolinas, he lost two brothers to British troops in the Revolutionary War and was orphaned at fifteen. With little in the way of a formal education and not much family support to speak of except for a small inheritance that supported him through some lean years, Jackson made his own way in the world after

ANDREW JACKSON: "INDIAN FIGHTER"

———◦◦◦◦◦———

In 1811, Shawnee chief Tecumseh called for a confederation of southern Indian tribes to drive "the white race" back "into the great water whose accursed waves brought them to our shores." Two years later, a Creek war party known as the "Red Sticks" took revenge on a group of white and mixed-blood Creek allies who had recently attacked them and were sheltered at Fort Mims in Alabama. In the resulting attack, about 250 to 400 settlers and militiamen died, not including the deaths suffered by the Red Sticks. The next round of violence was led by Jackson, who issued a call to arms to his fellow "Brave Tennesseans," warning that a "savage foe" was advancing "with their scalping knives unsheathed, to butcher your wives and children, and your helpless babes."[3] Jackson's force of regular soldiers, volunteer militia, and Indian allies slashed through Creek lands, ultimately crushing the Red Sticks in 1814 at the Battle of Horseshoe Bend, another lopsided massacre. In the resulting Treaty of Fort Jackson, the Creek Nation ceded 22 million acres in Alabama and Georgia to the United States, including land belonging to Creeks or other Indians who had no part in fighting with the Red Sticks. Jackson built a reputation as a great "Indian fighter" who gave no quarter to the tribes whom the expanding country was determined to drive west.

that bruising childhood. A proud, pugnacious, and easily insulted man who was far cleverer and better read than his detractors would claim, he was duly proud of his own achievements.

Like Abraham Lincoln, Jackson saved himself from a life of subsistence farming by studying and practicing law. Unlike Lincoln, he bought enslaved people at an early age (eventually owning ninety-five by the time of his presidency), participated in his first duel at the age of twenty-one, and was a war hero before running for the presidency.

After marrying Rachel Donelson Robards, Jackson parlayed her prominent Nashville family's connections into a successful business career and a life as a wealthy plantation owner. Jackson became a judge, attorney general, Tennessee's first congressman, and (briefly) a senator. Despite a gentlemanly demeanor, he kept up a long list of feuds, nearly dueling Tennessee's governor, and shooting Charles Dickinson dead in an 1806 duel (Dickinson's bullet stayed in Jackson's chest). In 1813, Jackson was shot in the shoulder after charging at Thomas Hart Benton—a future U.S. senator whose brother happened to be feuding with Jackson. While threatening Benton with a whip, Jackson supposedly shouted: "Now, you damned rascal, I am going to punish you. Defend yourself!"[4]

That pugnacity served Jackson well in war. Nicknamed "Old Hickory" for his staunch leadership of militia troops early in the War of 1812, Jackson gained broader fame for crushing the Creek Nation in 1814 (see sidebar, page 22) and was made a major general in the U.S. Army. His claim to immortality was solidified in the fall of 1814, when a British fleet tried to seize the strategic port of New Orleans. Jackson raced to the city and raised an irregular force that included white volunteers, Choctaw Indians, former enslaved people, and the pirate Jean Lafitte. In January 1815, the larger British force suffered devastating losses in frontal assaults on Jackson's hastily built positions. The tragic irony was that all the casualties suffered that day were pointless, as the war-ending Treaty of Ghent had already been signed in December of 1814.

The hero of the Battle of New Orleans then turned his attention back to solidifying American control over the southeast. Determined to drive Indian tribes and European powers out of the region, he led an assault on Seminoles who had been raiding American territory from Spanish-held Florida. While initially controversial, Jackson's decision to just take all of Florida was soon moot. A treaty negotiated with Spain by Jackson's future rival, then Secretary of State John Quincy Adams, secured Florida as American land.

Riding a wave of popularity in the 1824 presidential campaign, Jackson won a plurality of popular and electoral votes. However, no candidate won a majority of electoral votes (the requirement for winning the presidency), so the election was decided by the House of Representatives, and Adams came out on top. Seething over his loss, Jackson wasted no time in plotting his revenge. In October 1825, he resigned from the Senate and was nominated as a presidential candidate by the Tennessee state legislature.

JOHN QUINCY ADAMS

No more physically prepossessing than his heavy-set father John Adams, John Quincy Adams did not look as much the formidable leader as Jackson. His background as a well-schooled and widely traveled diplomat with impeccable Revolutionary family credentials did not count for as much in the new era of populism building steam in the 1820s.

Adams was a serious-minded, idealistic, and cosmopolitan youth, who took his first trip to Europe as an eleven-year-old in 1778, when his father was made the minister to France. After studying Latin and Greek as a teenager at the University of Leiden in Holland, the younger Adams served as private secretary to the American envoy to Russia.

Returning to America as a somewhat renowned junior diplomat (though oddly, his diplomatic repertoire did not include the ability to make small talk), Adams graduated from Harvard and started a career that followed in his father's footsteps: incisive political commentary paired with a sharp legal mind. George Washington, one of his biggest admirers, appointed Adams to another foreign posting, minister to the Netherlands.

Appointed by the Massachusetts legislature to a vacant U.S. Senate seat in 1803, Adams served five years before being recalled and replaced by a more loyal Federalist. Adams had committed the sin of supporting party rival Thomas Jefferson, whom he had always admired. He spent the next couple decades working in the Democratic-Republican party, serving again as a diplomat (including negotiating the Treaty of Ghent while Jackson was fighting in the swamps of Louisiana) and eventually as Secretary of State for James Monroe.

Despite having shifted his party affiliation to Democratic-Republican, Adams was not a good fit for the populist energies sweeping through the nation. After winning the presidency in 1824, he focused on a federal infrastructure program designed to improve the internal flow of people and goods. This program was seen by many Democratic-Republicans as a quasi-Hamiltonian move to centralize federal and Northern power. A further irritant to the South was the 1825 completion of the Erie Canal, which cemented New York City's status as the nation's economic powerhouse. Adams' infrastructure plan was ultimately at odds with a restive population looking to flex its muscles against Europeans and Indians while simultaneously hewing to an idealized and nostalgic national self-image of being hardy frontiersmen.

Blocked in many cases by an obstructionist Congress, suffering the death of his father in 1826, and savaged by the press, Adams spent much of his presidency in a depression. Despite the many improvements he had built, the fact that he blocked Russia from pushing into the Northwest, and his cementing of the Western border with Canada, Adams was never a popular president.

Jackson, on the other hand, with his dashing, gentleman-warrior image, unerring sense for popular sentiment, and rough-hewn, Indian-fighter bona fides, was a ready-made vessel for the young nation's burgeoning belligerence.

THE ELECTION

In 1825, the Democratic-Republican Party splintered. The 1828 election saw the American democracy returning to its usual state, which Alexis de Tocqueville defined as always being divided between two factions, "the one tending to limit, the other to extend indefinitely, the power of the people."[5]

Jackson picked up the mantle of the old Democratic-Republicans as part of the "Jacksonian" Democratic Party, whose ideals were primarily centered around a love of their fiery namesake, mistrust of government spending and the ever-controversial Bank of the United States, and support for slavery. It was comprised of a broad coalition of voters from the South and West along with a New York cohort, all held together by Sen. Martin Van Buren of New York, the savvy and somewhat ruthless political operator who helped unite the party around opposition to Adams' purported crypto-Federalism.

Jackson's running mate was John C. Calhoun, already serving as vice president to Adams, with whom he shared friendship but few opinions. A paragon of Old South stubbornness and an ardent foe of the abolition of slavery, Calhoun was a career politician whose views had shifted from Hamiltonian nationalism to near-fanatical states' rights advocacy that would later help fuel the Civil War.

Facing them was the incumbent Adams, running with his treasury secretary Richard Rush on the ticket of the relatively new National Republican Party, which reconstituted the Jeffersonian faction under Adams' less-than-enthusiastic leadership. Against Jackson's demands to sweep away the old order and return power to the people, Adams' sensible but complicated programs seemed wan by comparison and harder to communicate to a growing population in an expanding nation.

Still holding to the traditions of the time, neither candidate campaigned for the office. But, true to Adams' reserved demeanor and sublime indifference to popularity or making allies,[6] his campaign was decidedly less energetic. Unconvinced of his chances for success, he did not even act against those in his administration who openly opposed him.

That did not stop Adams' supporters from labeling Jackson's wife a bigamist and printing graphic "coffin handbills" that claimed Jackson had not only massacred unarmed Indians (likely true) but also showed "his cannibal propensities" by eating the bodies (likely not true).[7] The *Cincinnati Gazette* hyperventilated that "Jackson's mother was a COMMON PROSTITUTE" who "married a MULATTO MAN, with whom she had several children, of which General JACKSON IS ONE!"[8] In the ugly campaign, Jackson's backers returned fire and then some, accusing Adams of gambling in the White

House, misusing public funds, being a closet monarchist, swimming nude in the Potomac, and having "offered the sexual services of a young American girl to the Tsar of Russia while living in St. Petersburg."[9]

Hyperbole aside, Jackson's campaign had the better narrative. Given Adams' reserve, famous pedigree, and struggles to pass legislation, it was easy to portray him as an aloof and ineffective elite who was no match for Jackson's brawny frontier individualism.

Riding a vast wave of new voters—27 percent of eligible white men (women and people of other races were still denied suffrage) voted in 1824; by 1828 it was 57 percent[10]—Jackson beat Adams in a landslide that saw the incumbent only pick up a small portion of electors in the Northeast.

Jackson's victory signaled a transition from the courtlier first generation of American leaders to a newer breed of politicians increasingly in thrall to what they thought was the will of the people, many of whom were now living in the newer states to the West. Those people wanted the country to grow. They wanted the government to both help and stay out of the way. .

So did Jackson.

THE AFTERMATH

If the average American student remembers anything about Andrew Jackson, it is what happened at the White House following the inauguration on March 4, 1829. Adams stayed home, seeing no reason to play nice after such a bruising contest. True to the impulses of the Jacksonians, the party was no ticketed affair but an unplanned chaotic bash. The crowds were far bigger than anticipated, with fans of the new president swarming through his new house, damaging the furniture, and swilling spiked punch. The president had to be protected from the crushing mob of admirers. Afterwards, the stridently anti-Jacksonian *New York Spectator* sniffed about what the new democracy looked like: "Here was the corpulent epicure grunting and sweating for breath."[11]

Although this was the most vivid moment of Jackson's two terms in office—he easily beat the National Republicans' Henry Clay in 1832—other events had far more impact. Convinced he had been elected to save the American people from a corrupt and anti-democratic elite, he was determined (counterintuitively) to push the limits of executive power. Like many purported populist saviors, Jackson devolved into the kind of thin-skinned demagogue who mistakes an electoral victory for divine writ.

He started off with a campaign to replace nearly a tenth of federal officials. Now de rigueur, then it was an unprecedented nod to the partisan "spoils system" and led critics to charge Jackson was filling government with his hacks under the guise of "reform." What Washington did not yet realize was that Jackson sought loyalty for a reason: He intended to do precisely as he wanted, with as few impediments as possible.

One of his highest priorities was enshrined in the Indian Removal Act of 1830. Jackson believed Indians could never be trusted and needed to "ere long disappear."

His quasi-genocidal rhetoric had little opposition from voters, who were feeling the first flush of American expansionism and thought nothing should stand in their way.

Theoretically, the Act authorized the president to offer tribes payment and land west of the Mississippi in exchange for their moving. But the tribes who left voluntarily were later mostly run off their new land anyway. The roughly 100,000 who declined to leave were driven out by the military in the 1830s. Thousands died during the forced march to Oklahoma known as the "Trail of Tears."

There have been attempts to rehabilitate Jackson's image and make him seem more than an Indian-hating demagogue. But his ethnic cleansing authorization was clearly a central priority (perhaps in part due to the money he made speculating on lands seized from Indians[12]), since it was the only significant legislation he passed during his presidency.

Two other notable events in the Jackson administration involved muscular exertions of executive authority, though in different ways.

In the Bank War, Jackson's hatred of the federally chartered Bank of the United States came to a head. Having railed for years against the institution as an unconstitutional "monster" and a "hydra of corruption," he vetoed the renewal of its charter in 1832. This strike against perceived cronyism helped win him reelection and effectively killed Alexander Hamilton's dream of a central bank. Jackson was censured by the Senate for pulling government funds from the Bank, but the censure was later expunged after a campaign led by Senator Thomas Hart

Benton, who had become a staunch Jackson ally in the years since the two exchanged gunfire.

During the Nullification Crisis of 1832, South Carolina denied the federal government's right to impose tariffs. This was a new twist on an old Jeffersonian theory that claimed states could "nullify" laws they believed unconstitutional. Normally in sync with Southern state governments, Jackson was happy to use federal power when it suited him (such as when he asked Congress in 1835 to outlaw the mailing of abolitionist literature). When Jackson denounced nullification as treason, and South Carolina backed down, he temporarily helped preserve the Union.

Adams came into his own as a politician only after leaving the White House. During his nine terms in Congress, Adams was the body's most vehement abolitionist. In 1841, he successfully defended the Africans kidnapped by slavers who mutinied on the *Amistad* and killed two of the crew, only to be captured again and charged with murder.

Criticized as excessively pro-Indian during his presidency, Adams despised Jackson's anti-Indian policies. His contempt for the Jacksonians' proslavery views and mob-rule populism helped inform the Whig Party (started in 1834 in response to the overreach of Jackson's executive actions), as well as the reformed Republican party.

Adams' opposition to slavery was as moral as it was practical. He did not believe that the country could go on as only partially free. The first Republican president, Abraham Lincoln, would later agree.

PARTISAN PRESS

—◇◇◇◇—

Like any astute politician, Jackson understood the importance of the press. Also, like many a president before and after him, he courted prominent newspapers to produce favorable coverage to keep public opinion on his side and drown out the opposition. But unlike other presidents, Jackson practically had his own newspaper. Founded in 1830, the *Washington Globe* showed a pro-Jackson fervor that seems sycophantic even by modern standards. To some degree, though, it was a natural meeting of the minds. After publisher Francis P. Blair met the president, the two found themselves so aligned on hating everything from central banking to government (the *Globe*'s motto was "The World is Governed Too Much"), Jackson "practically vibrated with excitement" and later counted Blair as part of his "kitchen cabinet" of unofficial advisers.[13] After the *Globe* fulsomely backed Jackson's reform agenda, he repaid the publisher's support by giving Blair the contract for printing the record of Congressional debates and was likely not overly concerned when his ally somehow failed to print anti-Jackson speeches.[14]

WHAT IF...?

The conditions that bring strongmen to power are well-established. Among those that cropped up during the 1820s were: Easily demonized "outsiders" (Indians, enslaved Africans); economic uncertainty (the bank panics of 1819); a charismatic candidate promising power to the people (Jackson); and a divided opposition (National Republicans, a fairly weak agglomeration that never delivered a clear message). On top of all the favorable conditions for his rise, Jackson was also preternaturally lucky: He once survived an assassination attempt in which both the shooter's pistols misfired.[15]

Given all that, it is difficult to imagine a scenario in which an unenthusiastic and depressive diarist like Adams would have stayed on as president. In the absence of a strong National Republican—the only other party leader of note was Henry Clay, and he was soundly defeated by Jackson in 1832—nothing could likely have stopped a Jacksonian Democratic victory in 1828. One could argue that Adams had only himself to blame for the stature of his rival.

Consider: President Madison had agreed in January 1814 to start talks to end the War of 1812, sending Adams as his chief negotiator to neutral ground in Ghent, Belgium. Discussions dragged on long enough for the British to burn Washington, D.C. in August. As mentioned earlier, by the time Adams secured a treaty on December 24, it was too late for word to reach New Orleans, where Jackson routed the British on January 8. Even though Jackson was already nationally known by then, his Agincourt-like victory made him the most beloved American general since Washington.

If Adams had finalized the treaty more quickly, there may never have been a President Jackson.

ABRAHAM LINCOLN
– vs. –
STEPHEN DOUGLAS

We, therefore, the People of South Carolina . . . have solemnly declared that the Union heretofore existing between this State and the other States of North America, is dissolved. . . .

—South Carolina's declaration
of secession

The right of a state to secede is not an open or debatable question.

—Abraham Lincoln

★ ★ ★ ★ ★ ★ ★

— The Candidates —

*President: Abraham Lincoln
*Vice President: Hannibal Hamlin
Party: Republican
Popular / Electoral Votes: 1,866,452 / 180

President: Stephen Douglas
Vice President: Herschel Vespasian Johnson
Party: Northern Democrat
Popular / Electoral Votes: 1,382,713 / 12

President: John C. Breckinridge
Vice President: Joseph Lane
Party: Southern Democrat
Popular / Electoral Votes: 847,953 / 72

President: John Bell
Vice President: Edward Everett
Party: Constitutional Union
Popular / Electoral Votes: 592,906 / 39

* = Winning candidates

WHY IT MATTERED

The 1830s through the 1850s were as fractious as any period in American history. Pre-Revolutionary War debates between Loyalists and Patriots appear civil in comparison. Like then, a war would ultimately decide systemic questions about America's future. Unlike then, there did not appear to be a unified class of leaders like the Founding Fathers for the nation to look to.

Reflecting the country's divided mindset, White House turnover increased at a rapid clip. Up through Andrew Jackson, presidents not named Adams always won reelection. After Jackson, the nation saw a series of single-term chief executives, two of whom died in office. Power was handed off from one party to another and back again. The string of often-forgotten presidents and elections following Jackson can be seen as a positive. The peaceful transfer of presidential power, which had been cause for worry earlier in America's history, became axiomatic through sheer repetition. But the lack of continuity was unfortunately well-suited for a period when it looked as though nothing could keep America from breaking apart.

Flush with populist fervor after Jackson, the Democrats won the presidency again in 1836. New York political mastermind Martin Van Buren, Jackson's second vice president and one of the most trusted members of his "kitchen cabinet," pledged to continue Jackson's policies. But although Van Buren's victory was decisive, anti-Jacksonian Whigs were gaining in strength.

The small, foxish Van Buren had been known as the "Little Magician" for his electioneering prowess. But like many before him, once in office he discovered that being president was a different matter. When the economy crashed in 1837, he insisted the government should do nothing to help. That, and his refusal to go to war with Britain after some skirmishes along the Canadian border, aroused public fury and diminished his stature. By the end of his term, he was referred to as "Martin Van Ruin."

Van Buren's loss of popular support doomed him almost as much as the groundbreaking campaign waged by the resurgent Whigs for William Henry "Old Tippecanoe" Harrison and John Tyler. With catchy songs and slogans ("Tippecanoe and Tyler, too"), the liberal dispensing of hard cider, and circus-like mass rallies, it was the start of modern presidential campaigning as entertainment,[1] a development that only ensured passions would continue to burn over the following decades.

The Whigs, fracturing in part from an inability to take clear stands on issues like slavery or the annexation of Texas, hit a bad patch that saw them jettisoned from the political landscape by the 1850s. After the sixty-eight-year-old Harrison died from pneumonia after a month in office, Tyler turned out to be more Democrat than Whig. The Democrats narrowly won in 1844 with James Polk, after which the Whigs took their last presidency in 1848 (due in part to a splintering of the vote for Van Buren, running this time with the short-lived abolitionist Free-Soil Party) with Zachary Taylor, who died in office as well and was succeeded by Millard Fillmore.

Two single-term Democratic presidents of little renown followed: Franklin Pierce (1852), so unpopular that after four years his own party adopted the slogan "Anybody but Pierce"[2]; and James Buchanan (1856), a whiskey enthusiast whose apathy toward corruption was matched only by his inability to manage crises.

With a new influx of immigrants who swelled Eastern and Midwestern cities and headed west looking for opportunities, America's population almost doubled from 17 million in 1840 to 31.4 million in 1860. The country grew in size as well. Polk's 1845 annexation of Texas kicked off a war with Mexico, which was defeated in 1848. Mexico ceded roughly half its land, from Texas to the future state of California. A new Congressman from Illinois named Abraham Lincoln denounced it as a scheme to expand slavery into new territories, showing that tensions over slavery underlay nearly everything on the political scene.

Whenever a new state or territory was added, the question of whether it would be "free-soil" or slave-owning started a new controversy. Despite perverse balancing acts like the Compromise of 1850 and the Fugitive Slave Acts (which made it easier for plantation owners to kidnap enslaved people who had escaped to the North), things tipped slowly toward the abolitionists. By 1858, there were seventeen free states to fifteen slave states. That imbalance was seen as intolerable by Southern leaders who believed (correctly) that in the long run they would lose political power. This fear became so extreme that in the 1850s there were Southern proposals to annex Cuba, Mexico, and parts of Central America as new slave territories to even the balance. These delusional ideas heightened the growing sense in the North that slavery was less an economic interest for the South than a fanatical obsession.

Partisan conflict did not confine itself to newspaper pages or the debate stage. Those stark divisions were acted out in the chambers of Congress, where members called each other out and violently followed up on their words. Congressmen shoved and punched, threatened each other with pistols and giant bowie knives, and brawled in scrums "while colleagues stood on chairs to get a better look."[3]

The fight between proslavery advocates and abolitionists turned violent outside Washington as well. During the "Bleeding Kansas" period of the mid-1850s, proslavery militias fought Free-Soilers in the new territory in an ugly, internecine guerrilla war that served as a warning of what was to come.

One ineffectual president after another failed to resolve the issue. In fact, a 2017 C-SPAN presidential survey of nearly a hundred historians found that of the ten American presidents they ranked lowest, six served in the fallow period between 1837 and 1861.[4] As Buchanan's presidency ground to its ignominious end, the question became whether there would be one America or two.

ABRAHAM LINCOLN

The newest iteration of the Republican Party came together in 1854, largely to put an end to the slavery question. One accelerant among many was that year's passage of the Kansas-Nebraska Act, which lifted the ban on slavery north of the 36°30′ latitude (except Missouri) enacted by the Missouri Compromise of 1820. The sponsor of the Kansas-Nebraska Act was Stephen Douglas, an Illinois senator who in 1858 faced an unlikely challenger for reelection: Abraham Lincoln.

Beanpole-tall at six-foot-four, gangly, and rarely attentive to his attire, Lincoln never looked the part of the president, nor did he sound it. (Contrary to how most actors affect a deep, resonant delivery to play him, Lincoln's actual voice was more likely high-pitched and even, according to one newspaper account, "shrill.") Raised on hardscrabble farms in Kentucky and Indiana, Lincoln worked on ferryboats and as a store clerk before teaching himself to practice law.

Bookish, chatty, and a quick study, Lincoln had a somewhat melancholic disposition but still made friends easily, which eased his early entry into politics. The ambitious young climber served four terms in the state legislature as a loyal member of the sputtering Whig machine. Calling himself a "lone Whig star" from heavily Democratic Illinois, Lincoln won a seat in Congress in 1846. His denunciation of Polk for engineering a fake border skirmish to spark the Mexican-American War cost Lincoln politically back home, where the land-grab conflict was popular.

Leaving Congress in 1849, Lincoln moved to Springfield, Illinois, where he built a successful law practice and told anybody who asked he had no further interest in politics.By 1854, though, he was back in: stumping for fellow Whig Richard Yates. Lincoln lost a Senate race in 1855, failed to win the 1856 vice-presidential nomination for the newly formed Republican Party (the Whigs had collapsed by then), and unsuccessfully tried to unseat Stephen Douglas as Illinois senator in 1858.

However, Lincoln's last loss helped secure his next victory. During the legendary seven debates the men held all over Illinois in 1858, Lincoln benefited the most. The debates were blockbuster three-hour affairs, with raucous audiences riveted throughout, and the transcripts were published in newspapers around the country.

There were stark differences between the two, with Douglas ultimately pushing for compromise on slavery and Lincoln insisting that America could not remain one country as long as slavery existed (as he made this clear in his now-legendary "A House Divided" speech a couple months earlier). The diminutive and comically big-headed Douglas, nicknamed the "Little Giant," received thunderous applause when he portrayed the towering Lincoln as a destructive force hell-bent on giving equal rights to blacks. While Lincoln disavowed this, he nevertheless declared blacks to be "my equal and the equal of Judge Douglas, and the equal of every living man,"[5] hardly a popular sentiment among the white population of rural Illinois.

Quick-witted, dry, and self-deprecating, Lincoln won widespread acclaim for the debates. His profile was boosted further after a February 1860 speech at New York's Cooper Union. It was so well-received that he delivered the speech in a rousingly successful tour that presented the lanky upstart Illinois lawyer as an alternative presidential candidate to prominent senator William Seward, who was well-known but not particularly liked.

Lincoln's surprising nomination in May 1860 was further helped by the Republican convention being held in Chicago,[6] which meant he was the home-state favorite.

The Republican Party quickly aligned behind Lincoln. He was an unlikely candidate for contentious times, given that his inclinations veered close to those of John Adams: Federalist but thoughtfully so, broadly abolitionist, and generally pragmatic while retaining the capacity for soaring oratory. The chief difference was that, unlike Adams, Lincoln possessed innate charm and deft political skills.

JOHN C. BRECKINRIDGE

The normally unified Democrats were unable to pull themselves together. At their April 1860 convention in Charleston, the party failed to agree on a candidate or platform. Northern and Southern factions held separate conventions two months later in Baltimore, another shocking inability to compromise that presaged the war to come.

The Southern Democrats put forward the somewhat reluctant John C. Breckinridge, Buchanan's current vice president.[7] A strong orator and dashing war veteran, he was never quite trusted by Buchanan and so passed his time somewhat in limbo. Northern Democrats selected Lincoln's old adversary and Breckinridge's previous ally Stephen Douglas, who had become persona non grata in the South after his Lincoln debate performance was viewed as insufficiently proslavery.

Adding to the spectacularly splintered election season, a fourth candidate was on the ballot: Former Secretary of War in the Harrison and Tyler administrations, John Bell was nominated by the Constitutional Union Party, which had been formed by yet more disenchanted Whigs as well as remnants of the Know-Nothings (the recently collapsed anti-immigrant, anti-Catholic faction also known as the American Party) in an attempt to skirt slavery as an issue entirely and keep the Union unified.

Ultimately, though, the proliferation of candidates helped ensure that unity was impossible.

THE ELECTION

The new Republican Party formed in 1854 out of fragments of the Whigs, the Free-Soilers, and some disaffected Democrats that came together largely to present a unified opposition to the Democrats' push to allow slavery in new states. Even so, the Republicans were not the party of abolition. In many parts of the North, abolitionists were viewed as dangerous radicals, religious fanatics, or sometimes both, as in the case of John Brown, the militant leader who lead antislavery forces in the "Bleeding Kansas" fighting and was demonized later for his attempt to incite a slave uprising with the 1859 raid on the federal arsenal at Harper's Ferry.

But even though the Republicans denounced Brown's actions, that did not stop Democrats from race-baiting during the campaign. As the only party to acknowledge

LINCOLN AND SLAVERY

—◇◇◇◇—

Lincoln remains rightly enshrined in American history as the president who freed the slaves. But that does not mean he had an uncomplicated relationship to the subject of race. In 1837, while serving in the Illinois General Assembly, he declared slavery was both "injustice and bad policy" but that abolition "tends rather to increase than to abate [slavery's] evils" and that Congress had no constitutional power to stop it. Lincoln frequently denounced slavery as "a monstrous injustice" and said whenever he heard a white person advocating for slavery he felt "a strong impulse to see it tried on him personally." But he still avoided acknowledging that only force could end it. The apparent contradiction of being antislavery as well as anti-abolition was not uncommon in the North. Lincoln also distanced himself from many abolitionists through his beliefs that blacks were not equal to whites. Leading abolitionist and formerly enslaved person Frederick Douglass criticized Lincoln in 1862 for moving slowly on slavery and being as great a "miserable tool of traitors" as his predecessor Buchanan. But in later years, Lincoln's wartime evolution toward a more absolutist stance caused Douglass to believe that the president, despite his faults, "in his heart of hearts . . . loathed and hated slavery."[8]

the moral ignominy of slavery and state outright that they would use the power of the federal government, if not to actively stop slavery where it already existed (something Lincoln stayed quiet about during the campaign, leading to much handwringing in the South), then to at least keep it from spreading further, Lincoln and his allies were routinely criticized as "Black Republicans." In the aftermath of Brown's raid, Southern Democrats viewed Republicans as attempting to convince the roughly 4 million people enslaved throughout the South to throw off their chains: "Keyed up to the highest pitch of tension," James McPherson later wrote, "many slave holders and yeoman alike were ready for war to defend hearth and home against those Black Republican brigands."[9]

During the election, only Douglas campaigned. The others sent out the customary surrogates. Despite wanting to press his case, Lincoln stayed quietly at home in Springfield, Illinois, and received delegates. There were attempts by the other parties to whip up enthusiasm for their candidates, or at least fear of Lincoln (including crude racist propaganda), but the Republicans mounted a more enthusiastic campaign, replete with massive rallies, barbecues, and speeches, much of it coordinated by Lincoln.

Due to a larger voting base (white male suffrage was now nearly universal), increased press attention, dramatic differences in policies, and existential questions in play, turnout on election day was massive. Over 80 percent of eligible voters cast ballots, the highest turnout yet recorded for an American presidential election. Diarist George

Templeton Strong called the election "A memorable day. We do not know yet for what."

The results were dramatic and yet somewhat inconclusive. Lincoln's insistence on message discipline helped keep the Republicans together. That, the four-way split, and Lincoln having generated little political bad blood resulted in his receiving the largest share of the popular vote. While Lincoln had a more commanding majority of electoral votes (though not a single one from a Southern or border state), his share of the popular vote only approached 40 percent.

The lack of a decisive mandate made for a shaky beginning for a president who entered office as the drums of war were already beginning to pound. Five days before Christmas Day, 1860, South Carolina became the first state to secede from the Union.

Lincoln carried the responsibility of determining what to do about it. Interestingly, the president he drew the most inspiration from was Andrew Jackson, who had set an example nearly three decades earlier for how to respond when South Carolina was making less sweeping but similar threats.[10]

THE AFTERMATH

When Lincoln was elected, he stepped into a maelstrom of chaos and uncertainty unlike anything faced by any other president before or since. It was not just political uncertainty, either. Threats against Lincoln's life became a torrent by the time of his inauguration. There was concern Maryland might secede, which could have prevented Lincoln from reaching Washington, D.C. On his way to the ceremony in February 1861, Lincoln was informed by an old acquaintance from Illinois, the famous detective Allan Pinkerton, that there was a plot to kill the new president while he was switching trains in Baltimore. A quick rearranging of the schedule carried a disguised Lincoln safely through.

The capital that he entered already seemed to be in a state of war. Many Southern leaders, besotted with notions of defiant chivalry and unable to conceive of a world in which cotton was harvested by free people paid for their labor, took Lincoln's election as a sign that there was no way out but to fight. One Southern newspaper encapsulated the level of debate by calling the new president an "abolition despot." The next few months, during which tensions mounted and President Buchanan dithered, came to be known as Secession Winter.

After South Carolina seceded in December, a half-dozen more states soon followed. On February 18, 1861, former Mississippi Sen. Jefferson Davis, who had quit in fury after Lincoln's election, was appointed president of the Confederate States of America. Davis gave a speech arguing that the breakaway nation was simply fulfilling the intent of the Declaration of Independence, which had since been "perverted." Three weeks later, Lincoln delivered his first inaugural address, in which he extended an olive branch to the South by promising that "Though passion may have strained it must not break our bonds of affection" and looking forward to a future when all

Americans would again be touched "by the better angels of our nature."

Lincoln's rapprochement was not reciprocated. Claiming sovereignty, Confederate states seized federal forts and arsenals and began building a military. The federal garrison at Fort Sumter in Charleston's harbor was blockaded and running low on supplies. Barely sworn in, Lincoln had to decide whether to fight and hold or abandon the fort, both of which would break his inaugural pledge to hold federal facilities in the South but not invade.[11] Trying to square that circle with the awareness that if a war was going to start, it would be better for the Confederacy to be the aggressor, the new president dispatched a relief convoy to the fort, promising that its warships would stay outside the harbor while the other ships delivered supplies to the starving garrison.[12] But on April 12, 1861, before the convoy arrived, Confederate forces began bombarding the fort. The war had begun.

Over the next four years, Lincoln combined calm deliberation and decisive action to lead the nation through a crisis whose magnitude had not been seen since George Washington, whom Lincoln had studied since childhood.

Early defeats shattered the Union's initial confidence. Washington, D.C., roughly a hundred miles from the Confederate capital of Richmond, Virginia, was hastily ringed with fortifications. While placating strife in Congress with deft politicking, Lincoln struggled to find the right general who could lead his larger, better-supplied but frequently outmaneuvered forces to victory. In the first two years the combination of modern weaponry and

Revolutionary War–era tactics caused staggering casualties. The Battle of Antietam in Maryland on September 17, 1862, resulted in roughly 23,000 casualties, making it the bloodiest battle in American history.

Yet nothing dramatically moved the needle until the pivotal year of 1863. In January, the Emancipation Proclamation became law. While only applying to enslaved people in Confederate territories, it gave an inspiring moral clarity to the war's purpose. In March, the Union began drafting soldiers to rebuild a decimated army. Then in July came the turning point: A Confederate army led by the seemingly invincible General Robert E. Lee was soundly defeated at Gettysburg, Pennsylvania.

Over the next two years, the Confederacy was slowly ground down by an attrition campaign powered by the North's industrial might, a blockade of Southern ports, and the stubborn tenacity of General Ulysses S. Grant, a dumpy-looking alcoholic with a knack for logistics. Lincoln's surprising gift for mass mobilization was matched by political shrewdness. He was able to wage war while balancing anti-war Peace Democrats ("Copperheads"), War Democrats, and the Radical Republicans (an abolitionist faction that helped convince Lincoln to enlist black soldiers) effectively enough to decisively win reelection in 1864.

Lee surrendered his forces on April 9, 1865. By then, in a desperate attempt to delay the inevitable, onetime actor and full-time Confederate sympathizer John Wilkes Booth had assembled a ragtag network of operatives to kidnap the president. When that plan fell through, Booth came up with a more audacious one: Assassinate Lincoln, his vice president Andrew Johnson, and Secretary of State Seward simultaneously.

On the night of April 14, Booth entered the box at Ford's Theater where Lincoln and his wife, Mary Todd, were enjoying the comedy *Our American Cousin*. He killed the president with a shot to the head. One of Booth's co-conspirators attacked Seward the same night, but unsuccessfully. Three weeks later, Booth was cornered in a burning barn and gunned down.

By then, the Jacksonian Democrat Andrew Johnson was president and much of what Lincoln and over 364,000 Union soldiers had died for was suddenly in question.

WHAT IF...?

Lincoln's 1860 victory was hardly decisive in terms of the popular vote. But his command of the Electoral College was large enough that he could probably only have been defeated by a Democratic candidate who could have placated both factions of their party while also appealing to Constitutional Union supporters.

In that unlikely occurrence, would there still have been a Civil War? The increasing radicalization of the South since Congress outlawed the importation of slaves in 1808, and the concurrent rise of Northern abolitionist fervor, meant that a middle ground was unlikely to be reached. Also, by 1860, many Southern leaders were openly pining for war. That year, Edmund Ruffin, a popular and semi-crazed secessionist who reportedly fired the first shot on

"O MY GOD! THEY HAVE KILLED HIM, THEY HAVE KILLED HIM!"

———◇◇◇———

While remembered largely in terms of plain yet beautiful oratory and the power of his ideals, Lincoln's presidency began with the threat of violence, was marked by the most savage bloodshed in American history, and ended with his assassination. There had only been one previous attempt to kill a president. In 1835, an unemployed painter with delusions (he believed he was King Richard III) named Richard Lawrence tried and failed to shoot Andrew Jackson. Even after this episode, and despite years of threats made against Lincoln during the Civil War, the only security provided was a rotating four-man detail from the Washington police. They were not a crack squad. When Booth came to Lincoln's theater box, the on-duty officer, John Parker, was not guarding the door. He was either watching the play from a better seat or still at the bar he visited during intermission. Nevertheless, there would be no full-time presidential protection from the Secret Service (which Lincoln had actually authorized the creation of, in an attempt to fight the then-rampant problem of counterfeit currency, the morning of his death) until 1901.

Fort Sumter, published a futuristic novel, *Anticipations of the Future*, in which William H. Seward was elected president on a strictly abolitionist platform in 1868, spurring the South to the war Ruffin and others fervently wanted.[13]

Would another president have responded differently to the South's antagonism? If the Republicans had instead nominated Seward and won, the result would have been an ardent abolitionist president with even less interest in compromise than Lincoln. If a Democrat had won, that president would have strained to find the nonexistent middle ground between slavery and freedom and briefly held off open warfare, most likely resulting in an increasingly hostile relationship and a de facto if not de jure split of the country into two nations.

It is difficult to conceive of a scenario that would not have eventually led to secession and the Southern seizure of federal outposts. It is also far from certain that another president would have had the intestinal fortitude to challenge the South's right to secede (Lincoln never called on Congress to declare war, since that would have recognized the Confederacy as a legitimate nation) and pursue a bloody multiyear struggle to reunite the nation.

Without Lincoln, there is simply no guarantee that the United States of America would still extend south of the Mason-Dixon Line or that millions of Americans would have earned their freedom. Slavery could have continued indefinitely, perhaps even to this day.

———◦◇◦———

★ 1876 ★

RUTHERFORD B. HAYES
- VS. -
SAMUEL J. TILDEN

The slave went free; stood a brief moment in the sun; then moved back again toward slavery.

—W. E. B. Du Bois

Let me assure my countrymen of the Southern States that it is my earnest desire to regard and promote their truest interest— the interests of the white and of the colored people both and equally.

—Rutherford B. Hayes

⟶ The Candidates ⟵

*President: Rutherford B. Hayes
*Vice President: William A. Wheeler
Party: Republican
Popular / Electoral Votes: 4,036,298 / 185

President: Samuel J. Tilden
Vice President: Thomas Hendricks
Party: Democrat
Popular / Electoral Votes: 4,300,590 / 184

* = Winning candidates

WHY IT MATTERED

Between 1865 and 1876, America went from fighting what some called its Second Revolution, to liberating millions of enslaved people, to seeing many of their hard-won freedoms stripped away.

The period known as Reconstruction started as the Civil War was ending. On April 11, 1865, Abraham Lincoln delivered a speech to a crowd overflowing the North Lawn of the White House. General Lee had surrendered two days earlier. Rather than giving a rousing celebration of victory, Lincoln discussed more difficult issues, such as welcoming states like Louisiana back into the Union. He also addressed a question that was far from settled, even in the North: whether to extend suffrage to black men. Lincoln said he would prefer the right only be given to "the very intelligent" and "those who serve our cause as soldiers."

That was still too close to equality for many whites. John Wilkes Booth was among them. "That means n----- citizenship," he reportedly exclaimed. "Now, by God, I'll put him through. That is the last speech he will ever make."[1] A few days later, Booth carried through on his threat.

But Booth's bullet would not have had the same effect if Lincoln had not replaced his abolitionist vice president Hannibal Hamlin in 1864. In order to unify Republicans and War Democrats, he chose Tennessee's Andrew Johnson, a proslavery but anti-secessionist Democrat. Lincoln's calculation and a string of Union victories may have secured his election in 1864, allowing him to convince a war-weary public to stay the course. If elected, Lincoln's opponent George McClellan would probably have sued for peace (the Democratic platform called for an unconditional cease-fire) and nullified the Emancipation Proclamation (McClellan opposed interfering with slavery).[2]

But due to the unforeseen tragedy at Ford's Theater, a Johnson vice presidency turned out to be a political maneuver with devastating consequences. Johnson might have appeared on paper like a good candidate for a postwar reunification that exemplified Lincoln's desire to "with malice towards none . . . bind up the nation's wounds." The reality was far different, marked as Johnson's term was by incompetence, petulance, and virulent racism.

Starting in late 1865, Congress began establishing structures to protect those emancipated by the outlawing of slavery in the just-ratified 13th Amendment. Under the guise of states' rights, Johnson worked to undermine those strategies. He vetoed the Civil Rights Act of 1866 and the rechartering of the Freedmen's Bureau, which Lincoln had set up to assist the millions of newly freed blacks as well as whites in the South suffering from the effects of war. Both vetoes were overturned. But true to his reactionary nature, Johnson not only issued sweeping amnesty for nearly all Confederates but also gave them many of the 40-acre lots of Union-seized lands that the Freedmen's Bureau was parceling out to freed blacks.

Johnson's attempt to rally support during the 1866 midterms backfired spectacularly. His personal attacks on Republicans included a suggestion to hang two Congressmen, and his other views were all too apparent: "This is a country for white men," he declared, "and by God, as long as I am President, it shall be a government for white men."

Likely encouraged by their White House support, neo-Confederate resistance developed immediately. So-called "Black Codes" were enacted throughout the South, restricting the lives of blacks almost as though they were still enslaved. In December of 1865, a half-dozen ex-Confederates formed the Ku Klux Klan, a secret society that used terrorism to intimidate Southern blacks and any whites suspected of being sympathetic. The Freedmen's Bureau estimated that the KKK killed thousands. Other terrorist groups like the White League and Red

Shirts assassinated pro-Reconstruction politicians.[3] In 1866, racist rampages in Memphis and New Orleans saw dozens of blacks massacred by white mobs.

In reaction, the Radical Republicans in Congress, led by Pennsylvania's firebrand reformer Thaddeus Stevens, embarked on the ambitious "Second Founding" to finally enshrine the Declaration of Independence's promises of equality in the Constitution. This resulted in ratification of the 14th and 15th Amendments, which guaranteed citizenship and voting rights for blacks, and passage of a series of Military Reconstruction Acts, which placed the South under martial law to enforce equal rights protections.

Johnson was hit in late 1867 with an impeachment investigation, the first in American history. Among the many charges of presidential misconduct were his failures to enforce protections of Southern blacks. While he was acquitted by a single vote, the trial did not help his reelection efforts.

The 1868 Republican convention, which took place in May as Johnson's trial was ending, gave the nomination with relatively little debate to Ulysses S. Grant, among the most popular men in America. The Democrats put up Horatio Seymour, New York's governor and a somewhat notorious Copperhead. Like Lincoln, Grant stayed in Illinois during the campaign, but Seymour toured vigorously on an anti-Reconstruction platform. Grant won a large majority of electoral votes, with a thinner majority in the popular vote, which was boosted by the votes of nearly a half-million newly enfranchised Southern blacks.

Grant's deep commitment to Reconstruction was in inverse proportion to his attention to the corruption that spread through his administration. While the South rebuilt from the war's destruction, the first black public schools opened, and black-owned farms and businesses were established. Reconstruction also saw a rapid growth in black political power, including the 1870 election of the first black U.S. Senator.

Upset by Grant's cronyism, his tariffs, and his military-backed campaign to crush the KKK, Liberal Republicans tried to head off his chances for reelection. In one of the stranger developments in American presidential history, the Liberal Republicans selected as their candidate the *New York Tribune* publisher Horace Greeley. Unable to win the nomination from Grant, Greeley then ran on the Democratic ticket.

Despite the late-breaking Crédit Mobilier scandal—a fraudulent stock scheme involving government funds and bribery of Congress in which Grant's current and soon-to-be vice presidents were implicated—Grant won the popular vote by a strong margin. Greeley, his mental state battered by the recent death of his wife and the loss of control over his newspaper, was institutionalized. He died before the votes came in from the electoral college.

Grant's second term was plagued by more scandals, as well as the ruinous Panic of 1873. At the same time, he kept fighting to hold on to the advancements of Reconstruction. He maintained a strong military presence in the South to guard against terrorist violence and voter suppression. To complaints about "bayonet rule," he replied that if white Southerners treated their black neighbors as voters and citizens, "then we shall have no complaint of sectional interference."[4]

Grant was the last president to fight for racial equality for nearly a century.[5]

RUTHERFORD B. HAYES

After the seemingly unending scandals of the Grant administration, by 1876, the Republican Party and the electorate were ready for Rutherford B. Hayes. A well-schooled Ohio lawyer, Hayes was considered a man of strong character. He continued the tradition of presidential candidates who made their living in the legal profession.

He was also a man with ideals. An opponent of slavery, he believed that the Civil War was a crusade for ending it.[6] Starting in the early 1850s, he supplemented his law practice with defending refugees from slavery. In 1855, he took the case of Rosetta Armstead, who had escaped from slavery while in transit. Hayes won Armstead's freedom, partly thanks to the stirring eloquence of his closing speech, which resulted in long applause from the courtroom. His hatred of slavery was a passion that likely supported him through four years of service in the Civil War, during which time he advanced to the rank of general and was wounded four times.

Convinced to run for office, he won an Ohio Congressional seat as a Republican in 1864. He then served three terms as Ohio governor, during which time he

STATES' RIGHTS AND RECONSTRUCTION

———◇◇◇◇◇———

Since 1865, "anything but slavery" equivocators have insisted on other causes for the Civil War, ranging from unfair tariffs to arrogant Northern "carpetbaggers," along with their argument for "states' rights" dating back to the Nullification Crisis of 1832.[7] One purpose of this argument is to cast doubt on the Union's moral purpose for the war itself and its attempts to rein in racist violence afterwards. The point is easy to disprove, though, given that many Southern leaders were happy to abrogate states' rights when they saw it as in their interest (i.e., forcing Northern states to return formerly enslaved people who had escaped through the Underground Railroad or other means via the Fugitive Slave Act). While the North-South disconnect contained multiple vectors that still resonate in the current era's more diffuse culture wars, the clash over racial equality was the point on which there could be no compromise. Many in the North increasingly detested slavery as a moral abomination, while the South depended on enslaved workers for its economy. Several states pointed specifically to slavery in their declarations of secession. This means that if Southern leaders had just not insisted on brutal forced servitude as a condition of remaining part of the United States, the other North-South disputes over tariffs, currency, and taxation likely could have been resolved without the deaths of over 620,000 people. Similarly, it stands to reason that the quickest way for the South to end military occupation might have been to allow blacks equal rights, including the right to vote.

pushed for black voting rights. Despite this long political career in a time increasingly marked by rampant patronage and graft, Hayes was viewed as scrupulously clean and upstanding. That ring of integrity, in addition to his dedication to civil service reform and status as a war hero, made him appear to be a solid choice for a party that was on its back foot.

At the Republican convention in June 1876, the eloquent and stately House Speaker James Blaine of Maine was the front-runner. But amidst a crowded scrum of mostly compromised nominees, Hayes stood out for his uncorrupted credentials, if not for his personality. Henry Adams described him as "a third-rate non-entity, whose only recommendation is that he is obnoxious to no one." Hayes did not win the nomination until the seventh ballot.

SAMUEL J. TILDEN

A Yalie who made a fortune in corporate law and real estate, Samuel J. Tilden was just as successful and learned as Hayes. As many prosperous New York men did in the post–Civil War years, Tilden built a strong relationship with Boss Tweed, the head of Tammany Hall, the corrupt Democratic machine that controlled most of the levers of power in New York City.

In a surprising turnaround, by 1874, Tilden had risen from the New York State Assembly to the governorship and was making a name for himself as a corruption-buster. His change of heart seemed all-too-convenient to some.

Nevertheless, Tilden convincingly portrayed himself as a straight arrow, in part by helping to bust up Tammany Hall corruption rings and sending Tweed himself to prison.

While both candidates seemed to be models of probity and comforting blandness, their campaigns and the election that followed were anything but.

THE ELECTION

Battered by eight years of headlines about corruption and neo-Confederate propaganda, as well as high unemployment and an economy that been sputtering since the Panic of 1873, the Republicans were heavily tarnished going into the pivotal 1876 election. Although the Democrats had not won a presidential campaign since James Buchanan's 1856 victory, they were now resurgent.

In 1874, the Democrats regained control of Congress. Almost more crucially, the party reasserted its hold over the South and challenged federal authority at every opportunity. Not long after reentering the Union, most Southern states quickly asserted Democratic rule. By 1876, only Florida, Louisiana, and South Carolina remained Republican.

Meanwhile, Republican support for Reconstruction was waning. At the 1876 convention, Frederick Douglass worried that the party's wartime moral clarity was fading into apathy. What did emancipation amount to, he asked, "if the black man . . . having been freed from the slaveholder's lash [is] subject to the slaveholder's shotgun?"[8]

The campaign frothed with overheated rhetoric as Democrats reminded the country of Republican graft at every opportunity and spread rumors that Hayes stole his soldiers' pay during the war. Republicans hurled charges of bribery and thievery at Tilden, throwing in the claim that he was a syphilitic drunk for good measure.

Despite Hayes and Tilden agreeing on many issues, such as civil-service reform and pulling troops out of the South,[9] and efforts to suppress the black Southern vote, turnout was among the highest in American history: 82 percent. But the result was chaos.

Early reports had Tilden with a strong lead. Sweeping the South and adding Connecticut, Indiana, New Jersey, and New York, he took 51 percent of the popular vote to Hayes' 48 percent. With 184 electoral votes to Hayes' 165, Tilden was one vote short of victory. There were 20 electoral votes in dispute, primarily from Florida, Louisiana, and South Carolina. There, Democrats had waged a particularly violent campaign of voter intimidation, which was followed by Republican vote-counting boards throwing out many Democratic ballots.

The resulting Congressional investigation was a high-stakes, close-run affair. Through the winter, Democratic newspapers bellowed "Tilden or War!" while President Grant put troops on standby and removed a general who had pro-Democratic sympathies. The commission voted on party lines to give Hayes the 20 votes, putting him over the top. To head off a threatened Democratic filibuster, the Republicans reached a compromise by agreeing to remove federal garrisons from the South.

Hayes was made president on March 2, 1877. Amidst grumblings over corrupt deals and "His Fraudulency, Rutherfraud B. Hayes," he was inaugurated three days later.

THE AFTERMATH

It did not take long for the effects of the 1876 election and the Compromise of 1877 to become clear.

Initially, the post-election mood was one of buried hatchets and reconciliation. Working from a basis of wishful thinking about the state of equality and democracy in the South, even hardened Radical Republicans made overtures of peace toward their Democratic brethren. In a sign of the widespread trauma that remained from the unprecedented slaughter of the Civil War and fear of another war breaking out, there was a public reckoning in which Northerners apologized for their harsh rhetoric and Southerners tearfully repented for their past sins.

In September 1877, President Hayes embarked on a Southern speaking tour during which he promised a reunification of North and South. In a speech in Atlanta riddled with naivete, he promised "my colored friends" that their "rights and interests would be safer if this great mass of intelligent white men were let alone." The reality of that promise turned out to be Hayes withdrawing the protections that had allowed Southern blacks to make any advances in the preceding twelve years and stocking federal positions with anti-equality Democrats, essentially ending Reconstruction.[10]

Despite Hayes' incredible claim in Atlanta that the previous six months had seen "few outrages" against Southern blacks, historians later pointed to 1877 as the year when lynchings began in earnest. In the next few years, judges and legislators stripped away legal protections for voting and equal treatment. New constitutions were written that legalized disenfranchisement and Jim Crow rules for the separation of the races.[11] "I consider the South to have been the real victors of the war," wrote crusading anti-segregationist lawyer Albion Tourgée. "They have neutralized the results of the war and reversed the verdict of Appomattox."

While paying lip service to maintaining at least some equal rights, Hayes was steadfastly opposed to intervention to ensure it happened. Later historians argued that given the rising hostility of the South and the reluctance of the North to keep policing those states still recovering from the war's devastation with a small and thin-stretched army, Hayes did not have much choice. Whether or not that is true, what is certain is that Hayes and the Republican party dismantled Reconstruction and left a barely freed people to fend for themselves under white supremacist governments eager to reinstitute slavery in everything but name.

WHAT IF...?

Unlike most contests covered in this book, the election of 1876 was consequential for reasons that had little to do with who ultimately won.

WAVING THE BLOODY SHIRT

In the dark of the night on March 9, 1871, in Mississippi's Monroe County, over a hundred hooded and robed Ku Klux Klan members did what they had been doing for years: strike terror into the hearts of people who were trying to make the post-war South different from the pre-war South. They surrounded a house and demanded its owner send out Allen P. Huggins, a Northerner who was the county's school superintendent. Furious about his educating black children, the Klan members gave him ten days to leave Mississippi. Refusing, Huggins was beaten almost to death. Soon after, a U.S. Army lieutenant supposedly took Huggins' blood-soaked shirt to Washington, D.C., where legend has it that Massachusetts Radical Republican Benjamin Butler waved it on the floor of Congress while calling for a bill to destroy the Klan. Though there is little evidence that this ever happened, the phrase "waving the bloody shirt" was coined by neo-Confederates and was used to sarcastically dismiss as hysteria or incitement nearly any Republican criticism of Southern terrorist violence.[12]

By 1876, the consensus among many Republicans was that Reconstruction had been a failure. Exhausted by the ongoing struggle for racial equality and with no easy victory in sight, many were primed to accept Southern Democratic promises about protecting the rights of their black constituents. Given this fact, it is likely that all other

Republican candidates would have pulled support from Reconstruction just as quickly.

The one exception who could potentially have made a difference, Oliver P. Morton—a Radical Republican leader who despised Democrats with a white-hot passion and was the favorite among black Southern delegates— was sidelined at the convention due to his poor health.

As for a Tilden victory, given how aligned he was with Hayes on most of the major issues, his presidency would probably not have been radically different. Marked by gradually pulling the country out of its post-1873 depression and launching the first effort to build the Panama Canal, Hayes' one term in office was as restrained as the similarly anti-dramatic Tilden's likely would have been.

A Northern Democrat, Tilden was no supporter of the racist atrocities his party condoned or committed. But his politically calculated criticisms were so mild that even Hayes (writing in his diary when he still thought he had lost the election) was concerned a President Tilden would be too weak to stop those atrocities from occurring.

The greatest potential contrast of a Tilden presidency is that, unlike Hayes, who insisted on not running for reelection, he may have stayed on. With the power of his incumbency, it's possible he could have denied the Republicans the next presidency.

There is not much reason to think, however, that this would have ultimately made a noticeable difference to anybody except party stalwarts, political gadflies, the candidates, and their families.

WILLIAM MCKINLEY
- VS. -
WILLIAM JENNINGS BRYAN

Your duty to the country is to live for four years from next March.

—Mark Hanna to
William McKinley

That's all a man can hope for during his lifetime–to set an example–and when he is dead, to be an inspiration for history.

—William McKinley

★ ★ ★ ★ ★ ★ ★

⎯⎯ The Candidates ⎯⎯

*President: William McKinley
*Vice President: Garret Hobart
Party: Republican
Popular / Electoral Votes: 7,104,779 / 271

President: William Jennings Bryan
Vice President: Arthur Sewall / Thomas E. Watson
Party: Democrat / Populist
Popular / Electoral Votes: 6,502,925 / 176

* = Winning candidates

WHY IT MATTERED

From the end of Reconstruction to the turn of the century, the United States underwent the most radical transformation yet seen in its short history. A rapid influx of European immigrants buoyed the economy and transformed the culture. The transition from a rural agrarian to an urban industrial society picked up speed. Driven from one false refuge to another, those Indian tribes not yet decimated by disease and starvation were crushed in the Plains Wars that ended with the 1890 massacre at Wounded Knee. The campaign to restore white supremacy to the South, euphemistically known as Redemption, continued to systematically rip out the advancements of Reconstruction.

But despite their pomp and circumstance, that period's presidential contests were staid affairs that did not reflect the tumult in the electorate. This was mostly due to a broad consensus between the parties. During the quarter-century-long "Gilded Age" of booming markets and industry, there was general agreement about governing. Democrats and Republicans followed laissez-faire, pro-business fiscal policies and continued the country's habit of paying little attention to foreign affairs. The executive branch had been somewhat restrained since Andrew Johnson's impeachment trial, with presidents leaving much of the heavy lifting to Congress.

Nevertheless, presidential-year election engagement remained high. This was despite the frequency of violence and open bribery (including the practice of "cooping," or kidnapping people, getting them drunk, and hauling them in to vote repeatedly), not to mention some less-than-efficient or -transparent voting methods (by the 1870s, two states still voted *viva voce*, shouting out the name of a candidate to a scribe instead of writing it down on a ballot).

But Election Days were both grander and more intimate than the modern era's televisually mediated contests. Up-close affairs featuring in-person electioneering and torch-lit rallies with food, music, giveaways, and barrels of alcohol, elections were often giddy, bunting-strewn parties that allowed a growing country still barely stitched-up after the Civil War to celebrate together. Even though the policy differences between candidates often needed to be artificially amplified by their media operations in order to heighten the sense of strong differences, turnout (at least among white voters) remained high, with between 75 and 82 percent of eligible voters taking part between 1876 and 1896.

Political differences often came down to regionality. One immovable force was the "Solid South," the white Democratic hegemony founded in part on black voter suppression, which lasted from the 1870s into the 1960s. From 1876 on, their center of electoral power tracked primarily with the old Confederacy and border states, plus a number of Northeast urban political machines. New York was the most voter-rich state and thusly the most targeted by campaigns; between 1876 and 1896, it flipped regularly between Democrats and Republicans.

Victory in bipartisan America favored the more unified party, and while the Gilded Age was primarily a Republican age, the 1880 election was an exception, with the Republicans torn between two mostly ideologically similar factions: the Stalwarts and the unfortunately named Half-Breeds. After thirty-six rounds of convention voting, the unexpected victor was James Garfield, a well-liked Civil War general and Ohio congressman with humble log-cabin roots and a strong bent towards compromise.

Given that the parties essentially agreed on everything but a protective tariff (Republicans for, Democrats against), the result was the closest presidential election ever, with Garfield winning the popular vote by less than

10,000 ballots. He was just a few months into his presidency, however, when Charles Guiteau—a delusional street-shouter and self-proclaimed "Stalwart of Stalwarts" who thought he was owed a civil service job—shot Garfield in a Washington, D.C. train station. Garfield died seventy-nine days later, making his running mate, Chester A. Arthur, president.

Besides a push for civil-service reform, Arthur did little of note. This left the Republicans underpowered going into the 1884 election, which they lost by another slim margin (about 23,000 votes). The first Democratic president since James Buchanan in 1856, Grover "Uncle Jumbo" Cleveland was a scrupulously honest but unlikely candidate who weathered numerous scandals (the term "whoremonger" was commonly used), had relatively little experience, and spent his first term focusing on doing as little as possible. He called this being a "preventative president."[1]

Despite winning the popular vote in 1888 by about 100,000 ballots, Cleveland lost the electoral vote to the more media-savvy Republican Benjamin Harrison. However, Cleveland then took the White House back in 1892, the only president ever to engineer such a feat.

But the more crucial development of the 1892 election was the appearance of a third party, the Populists. In addition to cutting off a respectable slice of the electorate (roughly a million votes), they represented the forces that would finally upend the parties' long, cozy political détente and make the next election hinge on more dramatic issues than tariffs.

WILLIAM MCKINLEY

Ohio lawyers were well represented in presidential politics. William McKinley was nevertheless a rare individual. He combined inexorable ambition and likeability, political savvy and unimpeachable honesty. An ardent Presbyterian and filled with good humor, he was modest, popular, a skilled consensus-builder, and possibly the only American president to be referred to as "sweet" and "kind."

McKinley spent decades advancing through the ranks of the Republican Party. He started working for future president and his Civil War–era commander Rutherford B. Hayes in 1867 and later helped Benjamin Harrison's presidential campaign. Serving five terms in Congress, he lost in 1890, when Democrats gerrymandered his district. He won the governorship of Ohio in 1891.

He was praised for helping the state weather the Panic of 1893, which some thought was caused by a shortage in the U.S. Treasury's gold supply. Populists argued silver should be reintroduced to the monetary supply along with gold, a system known as bimetallism that the government had stopped in 1873. Normally the province of economists, bimetallism was the burning topic of the day and heatedly debated by ordinary people. "Free Silver" was supported by many farmers, who believed it would reverse the devastating collapse of crop prices. The "Sound Money" position was pushed by business interests who stood to gain greater profits if the gold standard held.

With the help of his wealthy benefactor, Republican National Committee chairman Mark Hanna, McKinley easily won the nomination at the June convention in St. Louis. Solidly behind McKinley on protectionism and the gold standard, the party affirmed a platform with a more intense focus on foreign affairs than it had for years. It laid out a road map for America's forthcoming leap onto the world stage, calling for a reassertion of the Monroe Doctrine, an expansion of the Navy, the annexation of Hawaii, and support for "the heroic battles of the Cuban patriots against [the] cruelty and oppression" of their Spanish colonial rulers.

WILLIAM JENNINGS BRYAN

Still a child when McKinley was fighting at Antietam, William Jennings Bryan was decades younger than his Republican opponent and even more energetic than his thirty-six years would have suggested. The youngest presidential candidate in American history, the fervently religious and grandiloquently folksy Illinoisan moved to Nebraska after graduating from law school. Putting his silver-tongued rhetoric and debating skills to work in getting elected to Congress in 1890, he earned the nickname "The Great Commoner."

Emotions ran high in the sweaty Chicago hall that barely contained the 20,000 attendees of the July 1896 Democratic convention. The pent-up outpouring of anti-establishment animus made the no-drama Republican convention look like a nonevent in comparison. Eastern party leaders knew there was rancor over Cleveland's intransigence on loosening the money supply, but they were still surprised by the tsunami of protest. Among the Midwestern leaders of the Free Silver uprising against Eastern plutocrats were Illinois's pro-labor governor John Altgeld (branded an "anarchist" by the *Chicago Tribune*[2]) and Missouri Congressman Richard "Silver Dick" Bland. Wildly popular with the convention's populists, Altgeld was ineligible due to his German birth. Bland was knocked out of contention after a pamphlet referencing his wife's Catholicism made the rounds: "If you want to see a confessional box in the White House, vote for Bland."[3]

After a speech from South Carolina's new Senator Ben Tillman—in which the one-eyed, mad-dog racist threatened to go to Washington "with a pitchfork" to jab Cleveland "in his fat old ribs"—Bryan took the stage to deliver his "Cross of Gold" speech. The fiery stemwinder channeled economic pain into a quasi-religious crusade and used the establishment's insistence on the gold standard as a proxy for its anti-farm and anti-labor contempt: "You shall not press down upon the brow of labor this crown of thorns. You shall not crucify mankind upon a cross of gold!" Referring to "the spell of the gifted blatherskite from Nebraska," the *New York Times* reported that "the convention went into spasms of enthusiasm."[4] Bryan's nomination was secured, as was the Populists' takeover of the Democratic Party. There remained some division, with the Democrats selecting one vice-presidential candidate (Arthur Sewall) and the Populists another (Thomas E. Watson).

Besides numerous planks about Free Silver and other loose-money ideas, the Democratic platform also included calls for a progressive income tax, denunciations of "foreign pauper labor," and the somewhat rote support of both the Monroe Doctrine and the "heroic struggle" of the Cuban people that reflected the party's inward focus.

THE ELECTION

For the first time since perhaps 1828, class and equality were on the ballot in the election of 1896. It was the first election in decades that would potentially be decided by actual issues rather than regionalism and tradition.

For decades, Democrats and Republicans backed business over workers, who had started to organize unions to push against the inhumane conditions of a rapidly industrializing economy. During the 1894 depression, after President Cleveland dispatched federal troops to put down a crippling railroad strike in Illinois, several workers were killed. As governor of Ohio, that same year, McKinley sent National Guardsmen with Gatling guns and artillery to stop striking miners from seizing coal trains. McKinley may have been sympathetic to workers, but like Cleveland, he valued order above all. In describing McKinley's mentor, Mark Hanna, the *New York Journal* stated he had for thirty years "torn at the flanks of labor like a wolf."[5]

While the economy boomed, so did inequality. The bipartisan consensus on laissez-faire policies resulted in great monopolies like the Rockefellers' Standard Oil that created the kind of generation-spanning dynastic wealth more associated with the royal families of Europe than American democracy. Although the debates of 1896

hinged on topics like bimetallism and tariffs, those normally arcane issues were vehicles for the frustrations of a
populist backlash unlike anything yet seen in American
history.

Each side took radically different approaches. Bryan
barnstormed around the country. Covering 18,000 miles
in a few months, he raged as a populist prophet about the
evils of the gold standard, declaimed McKinley as a tool of
the capitalists, and demanded that the government inter-
vene to help the "struggling masses." All the while, Bryan
clamped onto bimetallism as an all-encompassing theme.
His campaign even produced original songs for supporters
to perform on the theme, with titles like "Dad's Old Silver
Dollar is Good Enough for Me."[6]

Bryan's massive popularity in the restive South and
West made him America's first celebrity politician.[7]
But his homespun, revival-meeting style, fundamentalist
streak, and contempt for urbanity were less popular in
the East, even in areas with strong labor factions who
might have wanted to hear Bryan lace into the fat cats.

Caricatured as out of touch, McKinley still had a keen
political radar. A fellow Republican once described him
as having his ears so close to the ground they were filled
with grasshoppers.[8] Accurately assessing that he could
not match Bryan at speechifying, McKinley opted against
campaigning, like many above-it-all candidates before.
But in a brilliant counterintuitive twist, his "Front Porch"
strategy had the voters come to him.

Engineered by Mark Hanna, the plan involved
Republican delegations traveling to hear McKinley speak

from his front porch in Canton, Ohio. They came by the thousands, were uniformly impressed by the humble and gentlemanly but affable McKinley, and spread the word back home.

In terms of spending, the 1896 campaign was unprecedented, at least on the Republican side. Persuaded by Hanna with scare tactics about the unwashed anarchists banging at the conference room door, Republican businessmen shelled out millions, primarily on campaign literature and surrogate speakers casting Bryan as a nation-destroying radical. They also splashed out for other innovations like discount train tickets to McKinley's front porch; "cheaper than staying at home," the *Cleveland Plain Dealer* noted.[9]

Although supercharged by Bryan's populist evangelism, the Democrats were unable to deliver a broad enough message that could overcome the skill of Hanna's brilliantly orchestrated mass-saturation campaign. Despite losing the South and the sparsely populated stretches of the Plains and the Northwest, McKinley still clobbered Bryan by more than 600,000 votes.

One of the most decisive victories in American political history, this trouncing had all the hallmarks of affirming the status quo. This was only partially true, in that pro-business Republican interests remained ascendant. What the country could not know was that, in beating back the prairie populist, the stage had been set for assassination, world war, and the rise of an empire—not to mention the Roosevelts.

THE AFTERMATH

As the nineteenth century drew to a close, the notion of a large standing military was still foreign to Americans. Heeding admonitions of the founders, armies were raised for war and quickly demobilized. After putting two million men in uniform to fight the Confederacy, America had barely 20,000 regular soldiers to safeguard a population of over 70 million by the time McKinley took office. A navy that had been one of the world's most fearsome after the Civil War had soon atrophied. None of this seemed to matter, however. After America pushed Europeans off the continent decades before, the oceans appeared to keep other powers at bay. The naval dominance of Pax Britannica tamped down piracy and secured trade routes key to America's exploding economy. Save the occasional skirmish along the Rio Grande, the north and south borders barely required watching. That would soon change.

On the domestic front, McKinley governed much as his campaign had promised. Except for raising tariffs to keep taxes low and protect domestic jobs, he was not particularly active. The events his presidency would be remembered for took place offshore.

At the end of the nineteenth century, Spain's crumbled empire retained just two colonies in the Western Hemisphere: Cuba and Puerto Rico. Cuba had been in near-constant rebellion since 1868. By the 1890s, Spain's brutal crackdowns had driven the population into pestilential camps where tens of thousands died. As the Cuban economy collapsed and Cleveland handed

IMMIGRATION

——◦◦◇◦◦——

Starting with an influx of Irish and German arrivals in the mid-1800s, when the foreign-born population was roughly 2 million, the rate of immigration grew dramatically. By 1900, there were over 10 million foreign-born people living in America. As the century wore on, the majority were arriving less from Northern and Western Europe and more from Southern and Eastern Europe. Many worked in the factories popping up in the rapidly industrializing nation or started businesses, often settling in ethnic enclaves that allowed space for an easier transition to their new homeland. Reactions to immigration powered American politics in various ways. Republicans often appealed to nativism. At an 1884 rally for Republican presidential candidate James G. Blaine, one supporter blasted Democrats' Catholic support as "Rum, Romanism, and Rebellion." Democrats sometimes sought votes from new immigrants to power their Northern urban machines. But such appeals were outweighed after the anti-immigrant Populist Party threw in with the Democrats in 1896. As the century closed, discrimination against some immigrants was codified in legislation like the Chinese Exclusion Act of 1882. No sizable political coalitions tried to incorporate immigrant voters until the Progressives of the early twentieth century.

the presidency to McKinley, American newspapers were filled with heartbreaking stories of the civilian toll and jingoistic calls to war. In January 1898, McKinley, after trying to solve the issue diplomatically, dispatched the battleship USS *Maine* to Havana as a show of force. On February 15, the *Maine* was ripped apart by an explosion that killed 266 and left only 94 survivors.

The explosion was likely caused by combustion in the ship's coal bunker and not a Spanish torpedo, as William Randolph Hearst's papers were screaming.[10] Nevertheless, a reluctant McKinley issued a declaration of war against Spain and called for 125,000 volunteers to enlist. Among the happiest recipients of that news was McKinley's Assistant Secretary of the Navy, Theodore Roosevelt, who had been mocking McKinley as "flabby" for his lack of bellicosity.

Spain's navy was quickly defeated in a couple of decisive battles. Within weeks, the war-giddy Roosevelt resigned, formed the "Rough Riders" volunteer cavalry regiment, and began storming Spanish forts in Cuba. The Spanish-American War was swiftly concluded. In less than four months, the United States had acquired its first overseas territories: Guam, the Philippines, and Puerto Rico from Spain as part of the peace treaty, and Hawaii after McKinley annexed it for good measure while conquering the Pacific. The U.S. became not just a world power with a victorious navy but also an empire containing millions of new subjects.

The lightning success of what Ambassador John Hay blithely called a "splendid little war" seemingly united a country wanting to rally after years of dispiritingly dull leadership and fractious regional strife. But the corrupting nature of imperial expansion—a foreign concept to the Founding Fathers—took little time to appear. Philippine guerrillas decided they did not want to be swapped from one empire to another and took up arms. By 1902, a quarter-million Filipinos had died in a savage war that Mark Twain said "debauched America's honor" and presaged later ugly insurgencies from Vietnam to Afghanistan.

The campaign of 1900 was a remix of 1896, with the same nominees at the top of each ticket. Bryan brought in Cleveland's vice president, Adlai Stevenson, as his running mate. Bryan added the cause of anti-imperialism, joining with critics like Senator George Frisbie Hoar of Massachusetts, who called the taking of the Philippines "the downfall of the American Republic."[11]

McKinley's original vice president, the highly competent and widely respected Garret Hobart, died of heart problems in November 1899, and New York governor Roosevelt was added to the ticket in the hope that his frenetic energy would help counter Bryan's. The cash-flush Republican incumbency campaign, buoyed by a healthy economy and the afterglow of a quick war, was a smashing success. Bryan lost by a larger margin the second time around, unable to even take Nebraska.

McKinley's second term was cut short in September 1901, when he was shot dead by an anarchist assassin. Roosevelt ascended to the presidency. America entered the twentieth century a radically changed nation.

An industrial powerhouse that could project military strength around the world, America had now defeated a second colonial empire and become one itself—almost by accident. It was also, thanks to Roosevelt's ambitious plans for everything from busting up monopolies to building the Panama Canal and expanding the national park system, about to utterly change the very nature of the presidency.

WHAT IF...?

An America under President Bryan is difficult to conceive, in part because there is no example to draw from. Other populists have come to power, from Governor Huey Long in Louisiana to presidents such as Andrew Jackson and Donald Trump. Like them, Bryan commanded intense loyalty from millions of followers, pursued deeply emotive causes whose idiosyncrasy defied the creation of a coherent or lasting ideology, and was never afraid to stir up the mob to defend a very narrow sense of what America *should* be. But Bryan was never the chief executive of a state or nation, leaving to guesswork what kind of leader he would have been.

One constant in Bryan's fulminations was his commitment to anti-imperialism (Philippine independence was a major part of his 1900 campaign) and pacifism. A President Bryan would almost certainly have found a way out of conflict with Spain. Even the drumbeat of war from the Hearst papers would have eventually quieted, because Bryan likely would not have sent the *Maine* to Havana in the first place. Although it is entirely possible that a force of nature like Roosevelt would have found a way to the White House anyway, perhaps he wouldn't have been vaulted into hero status without the Spanish-American War, thus reducing the chances McKinley would have selected him as vice president and thus depriving him of the advantage of running as an incumbent. America's expansion into the Pacific would have likely been delayed, possibly reducing the chances of sparking conflict with Japan during World War II.[12]

In some ways, a militaristic lashing-out was inevitable. By the end of the nineteenth century, America had fully conquered the West, was bursting with wealth and industrial potential that had built broad political unity, and for the first time in its history had no frontiers to hurl itself against. But while these pent-up energies were bound to erupt somehow, they might have taken an entirely different path.

★ ★ ★ **1932** ★ ★ ★

FRANKLIN DELANO ROOSEVELT
- VS. -
HERBERT HOOVER

Meeting Franklin Roosevelt was like open-ing your first bottle of champagne; knowing him was like drinking it.

—Winston Churchill

If I fail, I shall be the last one.

—Franklin Delano Roosevelt

★ ★ ★ ★ ★ ★ ★

— The Candidates —

*President: Franklin Delano Roosevelt
*Vice President: John Nance Garner
Party: Democrat
Popular / Electoral Votes: 22,821,857 / 472

President: Herbert Hoover
Vice President: Charles Curtis
Party: Republican
Popular / Electoral Votes: 15,761,841 / 59

President: Norman Thomas
Vice President: James H. Maurer
Party: Socialist
Popular / Electoral Votes: 884,781 / 0

* = Winning candidates

WHY IT MATTERED

If he had run for the presidency two or three decades earlier, Franklin Delano Roosevelt, the most popular Democrat in American history and the sainted symbol of many of its signature policies, could have conceivably been a Republican. That is because, at the dawn of the twentieth century, the Republican Party, while having largely abandoned the cause of racial equality and deeply embraced the interests of the monied classes, still retained a reformist impulse. The first great reformer president, in fact, was Franklin's fifth cousin, Teddy. But the Republican Party that Franklin faced in 1932 was a far cry from the one that Teddy had led to a decisive victory in 1904.

Teddy Roosevelt's reforms—including labor protections, dozens of antitrust lawsuits, and regulations in food and medicine production—were significant and long overdue. His vigor and skilled political maneuvering resulted in many quick successes, boosting his already high popularity. It is hard to put a political ceiling, after all, on a man who once took an assassin's bullet in the chest while driving to a speech, then spoke for an hour-and-a-half before consenting to be taken to the hospital.[1]

But that changed after 1912, when Democrat Woodrow Wilson squeaked into the presidency. His bold reforms and new government structures—the Federal Reserve, the Federal Trade Commission, the Department of Labor, the federal highway system, labor reforms, and the federal income tax—made it clear that Teddy Roosevelt's vigorous executive activism was not an anomaly.

The reforms of Wilson's eight years are often overlooked. That is likely due to his entering the country into the faraway slaughter of the First World War (over 116,000 Americans died), the failure of his quixotic attempt to establish a peace-promoting League of Nations amidst the vast trauma of the postwar years, and the vehemence of his racism (reintroducing Jim Crow into the federal workforce, cheering the Ku Klux Klan, and mythologizing the Confederacy in his writing).

Even less remembered are the string of Republican presidents who followed Wilson. Taken together, Warren G. Harding (1921–1923; died in office), Calvin Coolidge (1923–1929), and Herbert Hoover (1929–1933) represented a return to the anodyne model of late-nineteenth-century chief executives. In that tradition, the president was there to keep things running on a macro scale, maintain a manageably small government, put most things in the hands of Congress, and not interfere even as the stock market ran amok and Prohibition-era gangs shot it out in the streets.

Harding, a nineteenth-century-style president who took unregulated capitalism and shady deal-making as the natural course of affairs, looked the other way while his administration was riddled by corruption scandals. A chilly Yankee, Coolidge was fond of dispensing statements like "[T]he chief business of the American people is business." When the stock market collapsed in 1929 and plunged the nation into the Great Depression, Hoover kept the government out of it, defensively claiming "no one is actually starving."[2]

During the same period, American democracy underwent dramatic shifts. Passage of the 17th Amendment in 1912 mandated that senators, still selected by legislators in many states, were to be chosen by direct elections, theoretically making them more responsive to the demands of the people. A more impactful change came with the expansion of political franchise, which for the nation's first century and a half was limited almost entirely to white men. In 1920, the 19th Amendment removed restrictions on suffrage for women. Four years later, Native Americans were finally guaranteed full citizenship and voting rights. Voting rights were still restricted in the South in a process described later as "a hijacking engineered through the trickery of the poll tax and the muscle of the lynch mob."[3] But even though Southern rural blacks who took part in the Great Migration to northern cities in the 1920s still faced discrimination (particularly in housing), their new-found access to the franchise made them important voting constituencies courted by urban party machines.

Having started the century with Teddy Roosevelt standing up for the little guy, small business, and the environment, by 1932 the Republican Party (and its grumpy president) was again the party of big business. Sky-blackening dust storms and foreclosure-happy banks were scraping family farms off the map across the Midwest. A quarter of the workforce was unemployed. It was not a good time to be viewed as taking the side of the capitalist chieftains against workers and farmers.

But only one candidate for the presidency understood that.

FRANKLIN DELANO ROOSEVELT

Raised by a doting mother in baronial luxury on a Hudson River estate and shunted along the Groton-Harvard-Washington pipeline of privilege, Franklin Roosevelt appeared to imbibe all the positive aspects of his upbringing (reveling in travel and the finer things) while sloughing off most of the negative. Beaming, chatty, restless, and wanting to emulate cousin Teddy's accomplishments, he had high ambitions and did not mind upsetting convention to achieve them. Although later denounced as a "traitor to his class" by the old Groton classmates[4] whose incomes he taxed and whose arrogant power-grabbing he denounced, he never appeared to let such combative stances dull his bright, sunshiny nature.

Born to be a dilettante but bored by a lack of purpose, Roosevelt ran for New York state senator before he was 30 and was luckily swept into office by a Democratic wave. After seven years as Assistant Secretary of the Navy (a job that seemed to run in the family), he signed on as running mate for the ill-fated 1920 Democratic presidential campaign of Governor James Cox of Ohio. In July 1921, Roosevelt was stricken with polio.

After years of grueling and ultimately failed attempts to walk again, in 1928 Roosevelt returned to politics and was elected governor of New York. Still filled with cheer and an infectious bonhomie, he showed new grit and resolve. Reacting to the misery caused by the October 1929 stock market crash, Roosevelt ramped up his progressive reforms as governor. Following reelection, he cast those reforms as direct attacks on President Hoover.

HERBERT HOOVER

Hoover was Roosevelt's opposite in nearly every way. Orphaned before the age of ten, he was raised by relatives in Oregon and worked his way through the engineering program at Stanford University. After years of international engineering jobs, he started his own consulting company and became a self-made millionaire. After leading a committee that swiftly returned home Americans stuck in Europe at the outbreak of World War I, he was chosen by Wilson to lead a relief effort that saved Belgium from mass starvation. His mixture of passions, combining an engineer's zest for efficiency and coordination with a Quaker-bred desire to help the less fortunate, made Hoover the go-to man to head global relief efforts well into the 1940s.

Coolidge's almost comically underplayed retirement from the presidency—at a press conference he handed out notes reading "I do not choose to run for president in nineteen twenty-eight"—set up his Secretary of Commerce Hoover as successor for the election of 1928. Promoted as a rags-to-riches success story and a magically gifted administrator, and despite being an awkward public speaker with a dust-dry personality, Hoover easily beat the far more colorful Democrat Al Smith. Even though he pushed reforms early on, Hoover's reputation as the wunderkind technocrat was dashed on the rocks of the Great Depression, a crisis his adamantine beliefs about government interference kept him from addressing.

Roosevelt had no such compunctions. Despite the irony of warning voters in 1928 that Hoover was a dangerous radical who would "issue regulations and . . . tell businessmen generally how to conduct their affairs,"[5] four years later Roosevelt promoted himself as exactly that same kind of radical.

THE ELECTION

Hoover was elected in 1928 with high hopes. But by his reelection campaign, the Great Depression had ground people down. Hoover's meagre attempts to stanch the bad news only made his public image worse. His sour disposition did not help much. Popular slang attached his name to all sorts of things no politician wants to be connected to ("Hoovervilles" for shantytowns, "Hoover flag" for a turned-out pocket emptied of money). Nevertheless, at a convention so sapped of enthusiasm that one delegate said, "even the nuts don't seem to care,"[6] the Republicans nominated Hoover for reelection. This was later read as either an act of desperation or a refusal to waste a perfectly good candidate on a lost cause.

The Democratic convention was more dramatic, with Roosevelt winning on the fourth round of voting after agreeing to take on Texas Speaker of the House John Nance Garner as his running mate. Compared to the Republican stay-the-course party platform, the Democrats had ambitious plans, which included Roosevelt's promise of a "New Deal for the American people."

Despite Garner's advice to "Sit down—do nothing—and win the election,"[7] Roosevelt hit the campaign trail with gusto, logging thousands of miles on the road. This vigorous campaigning helped burnish his carefully curated image of vitality. His wheelchair was never seen. Rather, in an artfully choreographed dance, Roosevelt gave many speeches sitting in his car and was frequently seen appearing to stand, only he was holding himself up by leaning on a cane and a supportive arm. He started filling in the details of his still vaguely outlined New Deal. In one speech, Roosevelt called for "distributing wealth and products more equitably."[8] This pointed to an economic interventionist stance that Hoover denounced as un-American communism, comparing it to the "fumes of the witch's cauldron which boiled in Russia."[9]

Except for agreeing that Prohibition needed to go, the candidates were a study in contrasts from ideology to style. Roosevelt's joyful ebullience made his certainty seem more confidence-inspiring than arrogant. In one photograph after another, he beamed out at the nation with a cocked chin, bright grin, and jaunty cigarette. Hoover looked sour and defeated, doing little but giving occasional speeches that offered no hope but plenty of the statistics he adored. Roosevelt's campaign song was "Happy Days are Here Again." If Hoover had a campaign song, few noticed.

When thousands of impoverished World War I veterans demanding bonuses marched on Washington, Hoover unleashed General Douglas MacArthur, who suspected a communist plot and drove them off the streets with tear gas, tanks, and sabre-wielding cavalry. One Hoover biographer later called the ignominious spectacle Hoover's "final failure, his symbolic end."[10]

Roosevelt won the election with over 57 percent of the popular vote and took nearly every state except a few in the Northeast, where Republican sentiment hung on against the emerging Democratic constituency of working-class Protestants, Catholics, and immigrants.

PRESIDENTIAL LIBRARIES

In 1939, Roosevelt donated his personal papers to the federal government and set aside part of his Hyde Park estate to house a future presidential library. Every president since that time has had their own library established as a combination research center for their papers and hagiographic museum-temple tended by faithful acolytes who skirmish with writers and academics who might portray presidents in less heroic lights. Ronald Reagan's library in Simi Valley, California, morphed into a massive complex with a hangar that housed a decommissioned Air Force One plane. In 2017, it was announced that the planned Obama Presidential Center in Chicago would contain no official papers, making it more of a museum and community center and removing the pretense of a library.

THE AFTERMATH

Roosevelt's victory in 1932 signaled the end of the Republican hegemony that had, with few exceptions, held the White House since 1860. Fittingly, Roosevelt would prove a transformational president of a kind not seen since Abraham Lincoln. By the time Roosevelt was out of office, an entire generation of Americans remembered no other president.

Roosevelt began the last job he would ever have at a time of dire crisis. The Great Depression's staying power had robbed the nation of its confidence and undermined trust in capitalism and government. Columnist Walter Lippman, who during the campaign had characterized Roosevelt as "amiable" but without many convictions, joked to the president-elect in early 1933 about the "critical" situation: "You may have no alternative but to assume dictatorial powers."[11] This was precisely what many feared: that the country would be so desperate for a savior that it could fall prey to a charming demagogue who promised he could fix everything.

Which Roosevelt certainly tried to do. His first few months in office were frenetic. He called Congress back early from recess and pushed through an extraordinary amount of legislation, including new banking and stock market regulations, labor protections, price and wage controls, and unemployment relief. There were also massive new job-creation and improvement programs like the Civilian Conservation Corps, the Civilian Works Administration, the Public Works Administration, and the Tennessee Valley Authority. After Roosevelt looked back at this period in a July 1933 radio address, it became known as the First Hundred Days, a span of time that has become a somewhat arbitrary and not terribly useful yardstick to measure the success of presidential administrations.

More programs followed, with a scale and nearly pharaonic level of ambition never attempted before or since by an American president outside of war. Roosevelt quickly transformed the federal government from a skeleton crew into a massive-but-nimble organization that launched program after program in an experimental, frequently grassroots-inspired rush of activity, shutting down programs that failed to work and pouring resources into those that did.

The success of some ideas promulgated during that feverish time—particularly bank account insurance (the FDIC) and retirement pensions (Social Security)—can be measured by their roles today less as radical experiments than as pillars of a stable democratic capitalist society. Many reforms (including laws establishing the minimum wage and abolishing child labor) were due to Roosevelt's Secretary of Labor, Frances Perkins, the first female cabinet member.

The president also bent an ear to his reformer wife, Eleanor Roosevelt, whose visits to one disadvantaged community after another gave him a sense of where help was most needed. A member of the NAACP and a vocal desegregationist, Eleanor was heatedly criticized for being too visible as a First Lady and not a meek White House host. Her advocacy for racial justice was often ignored by her husband, who felt he needed Southern Democrat support to get his New Deal legislation through.

Roosevelt did not end the Great Depression overnight. The remainder of the 1930s were marked by continued economic turmoil. But the economy improved in fits and starts, with the New Deal likely responsible for stanching the bleeding and keeping the country from slipping into chaos.

The swift implementation and comforting solidity of his programs made Roosevelt immensely popular. He was easily elected to a second term in 1936. Buoyed by significant support from black and Jewish voters, the beginning of a turning-away by those constituencies from the Republican Party, Roosevelt's victory was largely due to the belief of many Americans that their president was actively looking out for their welfare.

It was still a new concept.

But that popularity also made Roosevelt enemies among the ruling class and those who worried about the pace of change. Charges of communism and tyranny were hurled at the White House. A Jackson, Mississippi, newspaper worried that Social Security meant "average Mississippian[s]" would be paying for "able-bodied Negroes to sit around in idleness."[12] The animus was so heated that a cabal of bankers and businessmen, including future president George H. W. Bush's father, Prescott, reportedly drew up plans to overthrow Roosevelt with a private army and replace him with a more business-friendly autocrat.[13]

Domestic fascist groups like the Silver Shirts and the Black Legion cropped up in the 1930s. Taking advantage of continued economic trouble, anti-immigrant sentiment, and isolationist fervor often cross-pollinated with anti-Semitism, they found common cause with the rise of Mussolini and Hitler in Europe. In 1939, the Nazi-aligned German-American Bund rallied 22,000 fascists to New York's Madison Square Garden, where their leader, Fritz Julius Kuhn, denounced the New Deal as a Jewish plot.

The reactionary critiques of Roosevelt's emergency actions ebbed later in the 1930s. But as he approached an unprecedented second reelection campaign in 1940, a new crisis came to the fore.

World War II had broken out in 1939. But as the German Wehrmacht ripped across France in the summer of 1940, America was most concerned with staying out of the war. Worried Germany would conquer Great Britain, Roosevelt worked around legal prohibitions against providing direct aid by trading destroyers for land leases. His Republican opponent, businessman and political newcomer Wendell Willkie, decried the aid as "the most arbitrary and dictatorial action ever taken by any President."[14]

Staying mostly out of the campaign, Roosevelt got into the fray in the fall. Only days before the election, he promised in a speech that "Your boys are not going to be sent into any foreign wars." Whether a lie or just wrong, that claim was nullified when the Japanese bombed Pearl Harbor thirteen months later and third-term President Roosevelt (who had won reelection decisively but by a far narrower margin than in 1936) led the nation into war.

Roosevelt died in office in April 1945, just four months before the end of the war. Of the roughly 16 million Americans who served in the conflict, over 1 million were either killed or wounded. The economies of Europe were smashed, leaving America the sole untouched major industrial power. Due primarily to Roosevelt's swift, capable leadership, America had mobilized itself in time to give the British, Soviets, and other Allied powers the manpower and industrial might to turn back the fascist onslaught.

As Europe and Japan rebuilt, and the Soviet Union built a new global empire, America transformed by default and later by intent into the world's reigning military, economic, and even cultural power. George Will later wrote that when Roosevelt died, "America was more supreme than Great Britain after Waterloo, than France of Louis XIV—than any power since the Roman Empire."[15]

America maintained this status for the subsequent half-century of relative global stability later termed "Pax Americana." Before Roosevelt, Americans might have imagined their nation as powerful, but in a more inward-looking, Manifest Destiny, stay-out-of-our-hemisphere way. After Roosevelt, Americans took their nation's sudden, unprecedented, nuclear-armed, world-spanning power initially as a given and later almost as a birthright.

Roosevelt was only the third American president, after George Washington and Abraham Lincoln, to have exhibited the unique combination of strategic guile, relentless determination, and nose for public sentiment needed to keep the American people together at times when the nation's continued existence was far from a given.

Roosevelt faced not one but two potentially ruinous crises in the Great Depression and World War II, neither of whose outcomes would have been as certain with a different resident in the Oval Office.

THE IMPERIAL PRESIDENCY

Although some presidents before Roosevelt tried to expand the scope of the office, their efforts were often short-term and military-focused; Lincoln's radical war-time suspension of habeas corpus, for one. But Roosevelt's dramatic recalibrations of what the White House could do, and his still-unmatched twelve years in office, permanently changed the presidency. Post-1945, presidents were surrounded by larger and larger staffs, increasingly availed themselves of expansive concepts like "executive privilege" which were not spelled out in the Constitution, and were more likely to push back against Congress or act unilaterally when they felt it necessary. By the early 1970s, historian Arthur Schlesinger was writing about the rise of an "Imperial Presidency." Decades later, referring to the torturing of detainees during the George W. Bush administration, former Vice President Walter Mondale cautioned that when one president aggressively expanded their prerogatives, those who followed could be tempted to do the same. He compared it to "leaving . . . the loaded pistol on the kitchen table. Somebody might pick it up and use it."[16]

WHAT IF . . . ?

The standard storyline of a fun-loving Jazz Age (cue footage of stockbrokers, flappers doing the Charleston, champagne) ended by the stock market crash and the Great Depression (breadlines, Hoovervilles, and the Dust

Bowl) is a true story, but it elides just how close America came to collapse. Labor unrest had been building for decades, sometimes erupting in violence—such as the Ludlow Massacre of 1914, in which striking miners shot it out with the Colorado National Guard, resulting in 25 dead—unimaginable to modern readers. By the time Hoover and Roosevelt faced off in 1932, there was widespread concern that American-style capitalist democracy had burned itself out. Despotism, communism, or anarchy were assumed to be just around the corner. There were stories of the wealthy stockpiling food and weapons for when the seemingly inevitable revolution came.

Assessing what might have happened if a more run-of-the-mill president had been elected—if anarchist Giuseppe Zangara had succeeded when opening fire on Roosevelt at a 1933 rally in Miami—only to issue a few token reforms while leaving the system intact, historian William Manchester looked south and shivered. He determined that America would have gone the way of the "seven Latin American countries whose governments had been overthrown by Depression victims."[17]

Even failing a revolution or broad societal collapse, without Roosevelt, the twentieth century would have been almost unrecognizable. No American political leaders saw as clearly as Roosevelt the strategic advantage and moral necessity of fighting the Nazis *before* they conquered all of Europe. Without Roosevelt secretly pushing American assistance, an isolated Britain would almost certainly have fallen. Hitler could have then turned his full attention to the Soviets and, without the need to fight on two fronts, potentially defeated them. This would have left America with no powerful allies and likely still weaker without the twin galvanizing forces of the New Deal and World War II.

Nobody could have predicted that turn of events on Election Day in 1932. But it was common belief then that America was at a crossroads and needed a leader who could choose the right direction. During the February 1933 Miami assassination attempt, Chicago mayor Anton Cermak was fatally wounded by one of the bullets meant for the president-elect. At the hospital not long before he died, Cermak allegedly told Roosevelt, "I'm glad it was me instead of you."[18]

1964

LYNDON B. JOHNSON
- vs. -
BARRY GOLDWATER

Lyndon Johnson resembles an elemental natural force of some hitherto undiscovered sort—an amiable force, to be sure, not destructive like an earthquake, but still a very powerful force that is only subject to its own natural rules.

—Stewart Alsop

We have just lost the South for a generation.

—Lyndon Johnson

⟶ The Candidates ⟵

*President: Lyndon B. Johnson
*Vice President: Hubert Humphrey
Party: Democrat
Popular / Electoral Votes: 42,825,463 / 486

President: Barry Goldwater
Vice President: William E. Miller
Party: Republican
Popular / Electoral Votes: 27,146,969 / 52

* = Winning candidates

WHY IT MATTERED

There are many theories about when the Sixties ended, from the disaster at Altamont to the resignation of Richard Nixon. But that tumultuous period almost certainly started in Dallas on November 22, 1963. The assassination that day of President John F. Kennedy by a delusional ex-Marine, following years of seething panic amongst Texas right-wingers, put a definitive end to the media-managed surface serenity that had papered over tensions since the end of World War II.

Cultural forces roiling in the underground were ready to captivate idealistic youths who lost one hero in Kennedy and would lose others. The post–Civil War system of covert and overt racial discrimination was targeted for demolition by a new generation of activists. At the same time, the stage was set for the reactionary counterattack on the societal ferment that erupted after the first assassination of a president in over sixty years.

Kennedy's vice-president was Lyndon Baines Johnson, one of the Democratic Party's most powerful kingmakers. Mostly ignored and sometimes belittled by Kennedy, Johnson was perfectly placed to turn his boss's grand rhetoric into reality. In the dark days following the assassination, Johnson shepherded a wounded nation through some of its most painful passages, cemented his predecessor's legacy, and built his own. He also extended a devastating war, created the modern American welfare state, crushed pro-segregationist Southern Democrats, and passed more consequential legislation than any president who followed.

But to do all that, he needed to win a presidential election that took place less than a year after he took office, facing off against Barry Goldwater, one of the most curious candidates ever to make a credible run for the White House.

LYNDON BAINES JOHNSON

Johnson, a hulking and foul-mouthed six-foot-plus schmoozer from the Texas Hill Country, was like a photo negative of the man at the top of the 1960 Democratic ticket. Kennedy was the urbane scion of a New England lace-curtain Irish clan whose new-money roots had been neatly pared away by private schooling, leaving a brash and attractive up-and-comer whose telegenic chops helped compensate for a lackluster legislative record.

THE SWEARING-IN

Many people had tried to convince Kennedy not to campaign in Dallas. By 1963, the city had become a locus for well-funded Texas right-wingers pumping out propaganda about how Kennedy was a traitor and the Communists were taking over. In October, after being assaulted there by a frenzied mob while making a speech, UN Ambassador Adlai Stevenson wondered: "Are these human beings, or are they animals?"[1] On the flight in, Kennedy jokingly warned his wife, Jackie, "We're heading into nut country today." Johnson prepared a joke for the following day: "And thank God, Mr. President, you came out of Dallas alive."[2] A half-hour after being shot in his motorcade on November 22, 1963, Kennedy was declared dead. Roughly an hour and a half later, his body was loaded onto *Air Force One*. The plane was filled with anxious aides and Secret Service men trying to hold back tears while history happened around them. Johnson was sworn in as president by federal judge Sarah T. Hughes while standing next to Jackie in a crowded huddle. Lady Bird suggested to Jackie that she take off her blood-stained dress. Jackie declined, saying "I want them to see what they have done to Jack." A few minutes later, Johnson gave his first order as president: "Now, let's get airborne."

Kennedy's cool sophistication and aura of literate wartime heroism conferred by his best-selling book *Profiles in Courage* (1956) made a bright contrast with the bland old Eisenhower establishment represented by Republican candidate Richard Nixon. Still, Kennedy was a long shot. At 43, he would be younger than any other elected president. Plus, the last Roman Catholic candidate, New York's Al Smith, had been met with the Ku Klux Klan's burning crosses while campaigning in 1928.

Kennedy leaned into the controversy. He emphasized his youth, promised to out-spend the Republicans on defense, and assured Protestants his loyalty to America trumped obedience to the Vatican. Despite mocking Johnson as "Uncle Cornpone," the smart young Ivy Leaguer knew he needed a skilled old hand like the Texas veteran, who had been blocking civil rights bills practically since entering Congress in 1937, to make Southern Democrats less nervous about electing a Northeastern liberal.

Their differences in style, background, and approach meant that even after beating Nixon in the 1960 election by about 0.17 percent of all votes cast, JFK and LBJ would never be close colleagues. As vice president, the hummingbird-busy Johnson was sidelined by the president and his younger brother Bobby Kennedy, the new Attorney General. Johnson groused about both Kennedys, calling Jack "pathetic as a congressman" and reminding people that Bobby started off as Joe McCarthy's counsel: "It was like a rattlesnake charming a rabbit."[3]

Nevertheless, after Kennedy's death, Johnson was shattered. Whether the pain he felt was for the country, the man, or JFK's heartbroken widow, nobody knew. On November 27, the thirty-sixth president of the United States addressed a joint session of Congress. Stern and resolute, Johnson delivered a soaring speech that threaded many needles. It was at once a clarion call for unity in a time of tragedy ("An assassin's bullet has thrust upon me the awesome burden of the Presidency . . . I need your help; I cannot bear this burden alone"); an articulation of muscular liberal idealism; a plea to honor a fallen president by taking up his stalled legislative agenda; and a portrayal of himself as America's healer.

All Johnson's previously stymied energies were now unleashed. He had no trouble thinking big. This was a man, after all, who had declared he would be president while still a gangly teenager working on a Texas road crew. [4]

The torrent of activity that convulsed Washington through the first eight months of 1964 may seem incomprehensible to modern readers. On January 23, 1964, the 24th Amendment abolishing poll taxes was ratified. On May 22, Johnson delivered his "Great Society" speech in which he presented himself as a latter-day FDR who would complete the promise of the New Deal. He also laid out a sweeping vision for "a society where no child will go unfed, and no youngster will go unschooled." He signed the Civil Rights Act of 1964—which outlawed discrimination based on race, color, sex, religion, or national origin—into law on July 2, demonstrating yet again how his intense personal animus against discrimination overrode his white Southern political instincts. On August 20, he signed the Economic Opportunity Act, which launched his vaunted War on Poverty.

Earlier in August, Johnson had also found time for the Gulf of Tonkin Resolution, which set the stage for the Vietnam War. While furiously passing legislation to bring the country together, he also pursued a war that would tear it apart.

BARRY GOLDWATER

Facing Johnson in 1964 was a man almost as unlikely as the Texas arm-twister. The first modern candidate to hail from the rapidly suburbanizing "Sun Belt," Barry Goldwater was an Arizona firebrand so far to the right of then-staid Republicanism that he mocked Eisenhower's administration as a "dime store New Deal."

The scion of a Phoenix merchant family, Goldwater used his knack for self-promotion and quick wit to win a Senate seat in 1952. His anti-government vehemence was matched by a fervent anti-communism that frequently crossed into hyperbole. While his 1960 surprise bestseller *The Conscience of a Conservative* dryly defined conservative politics as "the art of achieving the maximum amount of freedom for individuals that is consistent with the maintenance of social order,"[5] his rhetoric plugged right into the hot, conspiratorial paranoia promulgated by groups like the John Birch Society and heartland screeds like John Stormer's *None Dare Call It*

Treason (1964) and Phyllis Schlafly's *A Choice Not an Echo* (1964).

Goldwater's anti-Washington hawkishness found a ready audience with revanchist Republicans. Their revolutionary fury was directed at establishment Republicans and, in a portent of things to come, the television media. Conservatives of the West and South made up a "federation of the fed-up"[6] primed for a cowboy-ish pro-business loudmouth who could feed their nostalgia for a fantasy of individualism—the closest they would get to an electoral John Wayne.

Goldwater vented their rage at government spending, the sense that the era of the individual was over, and establishment Republicans who wanted to play nice. They wanted Goldwater, the guy who mused about dropping an atomic bomb on the Ho Chi Minh Trail and who was described in the *Saturday Evening Post* as an "unstuffed shirt" who was "crazy about jet planes, Indians and mechanical doodads" and who blurted out uncensored thoughts like the East Coast needing to be "sliced off and set adrift."[7]

The same loud mouth that made Goldwater a star to his backers also undid him in an election that was never going to go his way.

THE ELECTION

Goldwater had lost the New Hampshire primary to the more centrist Henry Cabot Lodge, Jr. before clinching the nomination. In the process, he ignited something of a schism in the party. The momentum at the July 1964 Republican Convention in San Francisco's Cow Palace—a frenzied scene later termed the "Woodstock of the right" by Goldwater biographer Robert Alan Goldberg—favored the insurgents. They were furious at the grey-flannel-suit Eastern Establishment personified by Goldwater's only serious challenger for the nomination, New York governor and one of the wealthiest men to have ever sought the presidency, Nelson Rockefeller.

The anti-Rockefeller resistance centered on his support of Johnson's civil rights agenda. Despite the Republican Party's post-Lincoln record on the issue, the early- and mid-1960s were an inflection point in which party loyalties became scrambled. On a personal level, Goldwater was arguably more racially progressive than many Democrats. He was an NAACP member who took politically risky actions like desegregating his family store in Phoenix and the Arizona Air National Guard.

But those facts were lost on the white backlash contingent who cheered Goldwater's votes against the 1964 civil rights bill, even though he claimed to oppose it only on strict constitutionalist grounds. Just as he outwardly rejected radical Birchers even while garnering massive support from them, Goldwater's approach to civil rights required him to essentially profit from others' racism while avoiding being criticized for agreeing with their beliefs.[8]

While avoiding obviously racist appeals, Goldwater's campaign inaugurated the now-familiar "law and order" tactic of packaging racial backlash as respect for authority. Goldwater played to Jim Crow supporters and linked civil rights legislation to civil violence. At the same time, Johnson was aware many white voters were still uncomfortable with civil rights legislation. Johnson told his FBI liaison to put an end to one riot in New York after a police shooting because every such outbreak "costs me 90,000 votes."[9]

The extremist and moderate factions clashed explosively in the Cow Palace, where a wave of boos and shouts of "We want Barry" crashed over Rockefeller, drowning out his warning about the dangerous tactics of the "radical, well-financed and highly disciplined"[10] Goldwater brigades. As if to prove Rockefeller's point about the insurgents' habit of "threats of personal violence," an Alabama delegate had to be restrained from attacking fellow delegate Jackie Robinson after the baseball star and lifelong Republican shouted his support for the governor. Another black delegate had a cigarette put out on him by Goldwater backers. Robinson later said that afterwards he had "a better understanding of how it must have felt to be a Jew in Hitler's Germany."[11] After 1964, the Republican Party, which once shrouded itself in the mantle of Lincoln and emancipation, never received more than 15 percent of the black vote in presidential elections.[12]

When Goldwater took the stage to accept the nomination, he delivered just the kind of high-octane moral outrage his supporters demanded. Saying that "extremism in the defense of liberty is no vice [and] . . . moderation in the pursuit of justice is no virtue," he laid down a vision of how a divided party could unite itself, for better or worse.

Johnson sailed into the election with a message of unity, hope, and forward momentum: "All the Way with LBJ." Questions about Johnson's personal wealth and a quasi-comical scandal involving an insurance policy and a stereo were seized on by Goldwater's campaign but never took root. The president's approval ratings never dipped below 70 percent during the election, in large part due to what was termed "a martyr-besotted electorate."[13]

Johnson was pressured to assemble a seemingly impossible coalition. Vying to be the first president elected from the South in a century, he needed to convince Northern liberals that he would move on progressive issues, particularly during the drama and violent tragedies of 1964's "Freedom Summer" black voter registration drive. At the same time, he had to keep white Southern voters from souring on him for supporting civil rights and block Goldwater's nuclear bellicosity by building up his anti-communist bona fides. He pursued the latter in part by pressing Congress, following an alleged attack by the North Vietnamese on U.S. Navy destroyers, to unanimously pass the Gulf of Tonkin Resolution, which Secretary of Defense Robert McNamara described to Johnson as "a blank check" to prosecute what was rapidly turning into the Vietnam War.[14]

Johnson campaigned actively around the country. At the Democratic Convention in Atlantic City, he built a bridge to the party's liberal wing and disappointed

"THE GOLDWATER RULE"

The September-October 1964 issue of the political magazine *Fact* published some responses to the thousands of questionnaires they sent to psychiatrists. The questionnaires asked: "Do you believe Barry Goldwater is psychologically fit to serve as President of the United States?" Of the respondents, 657 affirmed he was fit and 1,189 said he was not. Among these remote diagnoses were listed concerns about "distinct persecution feelings," "paranoid and omnipotent tendencies," and "chronic psychosis."[15] The discomfort caused by this clearly unscientific survey led to the American Psychiatric Association adopting the so-called "Goldwater Rule" in 1973, declaring "it is unethical for a psychiatrist to offer a professional opinion unless he or she has conducted an examination." *Fact*'s story was a reaction to concern at a time of high anxiety over nuclear war that Goldwater's blasé, off-the-cuff declarations (e.g., thermonuclear weapons were just "a more efficient means of destruction") were signals of dangerous impulsivity. The Johnson campaign brilliantly played off this worry with groundbreaking attack ads, most infamously the "Daisy" spot. One minute long and broadcast just once, it starts with a girl counting as she pulls petals off a flower. The camera zooms in on her eye as an ominous voice counts down to liftoff. A nuclear mushroom cloud erupts, followed by an on-screen reminder to vote for Johnson. The narrator then intones, "the stakes are too high for you to stay home." Goldwater's name is never mentioned, but the meaning is clear.

Robert Kennedy by selecting as his running mate the Minnesota progressive Hubert Humphrey.

When Johnson accepted the nomination on August 26, it was almost a non-event. The same could be said about the election itself, even despite its accusations of mental illness, the threat of nuclear annihilation, and a near-remaking of the Republican Party. Goldwater's insurgent operation tried to work out a completely new style of Republican messaging on the fly and never quite coalesced. Even when not railing against the federal bureaucracy and promoting the glories of nuclear weapons, Goldwater mused about privatizing Social Security. All in all, he seemed too risky a bet for the electorate.

Johnson won 44 states to Goldwater's 6, retaining the presidency in one of the largest popular vote landslides in American history.

THE AFTERMATH

Ironically, the man who weakened the first Civil Rights Act in 1957 because he "wanted a cosmetic bill that would enhance his presidential ambitions without alienating his white Southern base,"[16] recast himself as civil rights champion.

Endorsing Johnson in October 1964, the classically centrist *Atlantic* magazine pointed to the hope that Johnson could reconcile "the vexed problem of civil rights" and prevent America "from stumbling down the road taken by South Africa."[17]

Johnson worked strenuously to meet these challenges. In 1965, the century's most prodigiously gifted legislator added to his roster of accomplishments the Voting Rights Act (outlawing practices used to keep blacks from registering to vote), the creation of Medicare and Medicaid, and the Elementary and Secondary Education Act (providing federal funding to precollegiate schooling for the first time).

Nevertheless, for all the progress Johnson made expanding the promise of the New Deal, the nation was fracturing under the onslaught of generational and societal change that would also realign old loyalties and factions and inaugurate a long period of political instability.

Part of that was due to the Vietnam War. In June 1964, the Pentagon was already running a strong counterinsurgency campaign in South Vietnam. Weeks into his presidency, Johnson authorized Operation Rolling Thunder, the devastating multiyear North Vietnam bombing campaign. In March 1965, the 9th U.S. Marine Expeditionary Brigade landed at Da Nang in South Vietnam, the first combat troops to enter the fray. By the end of that year, there were nearly 200,000 American troops in theater.[18] By 1968, American had lost nearly 17,000 troops out of a half-million on the ground. At home, a growing peace movement railed against the Democratic Party's promotion of an ugly, pointless war with a gruesome civilian toll. "Hey, hey, LBJ, how many kids did you kill today?" was chanted at Johnson.

Meanwhile, conservatives connected everything from protests to race riots, the violent crime spike, and a general sense of unease to Johnson's progressive domestic agenda. For them, the country was falling apart under a disturbing all-out assault on everything they understood as American.

Though Johnson won the election of 1964, it was a painful victory. For reasons ranging from habitual distrust of deeply accented Southerners to horror over the war, Johnson never won liberals' hearts. Because of his social programs and reforms, many conservatives viewed him as the textbook example of big government run amok.

Not long after the Tet Offensive shook American confidence in the Vietnam War's winnability, with progressive rivals like Robert Kennedy and Eugene McCarthy seeking the nomination, and Johnson's approval rating slumping to 36 percent, he announced on March 31, 1968, that he would not seek reelection. Becoming president had been perhaps the greatest driving factor in Johnson's life. But, scarred by childhood poverty and his father's boom-and-bust habits, his fear of failure was almost as pronounced, and it ultimately kept him from seeking another term.

For Goldwater, defeat was in some ways no great loss. He returned to the Senate in 1968 and was reelected twice. Despite his 1964 campaign's moral messaging, he became an outlier in a party whose increasing emphasis on issues like prayer in schools and gay rights offended his ideological libertarianism.

Conventional wisdom held that Goldwater's rebels had pushed the GOP out of contention for the foreseeable future. But his defeat actually presaged future victories for the party. He was later termed "the most consequential loser of 20th century politics," as Goldwater's tactics and extremism "disgusted Republican leaders in 1964—except one."[19] Richard Nixon studied how Goldwater turned anti-establishment anger and fear of change into a coalition. He drew on his own underappreciated political skills to make his campaign a winning one in 1968. In 1972, Nixon won reelection in a landslide almost as lopsided as Johnson's.

Goldwater's "In Your Heart You Know He's Right" campaign ad used street-fighting footage behind the candidate's prophesying that the "cult of individual and government irresponsibility" was "an insidious cancer that will destroy us." The mixture of quasi-Randian individualism, tut-tutting morality, and apocalyptic fright prefigured the "movement conservatism" that would come to dominate grassroots Republican politics for the rest of the century.

WHAT IF...?

It's hard to imagine a President Goldwater, given the lopsided nature of the 1964 election. But history is a slippery thing. Events that seem preordained afterwards were generally far more fungible in the present. One factor that could have nudged Goldwater to victory would have been a continuance of the riots that ripped through American cities in the summer of 1964. If the Republicans had capitalized on that and sewn distrust of Johnson's proposed agenda, Nixon's "silent majority" coalition could have formed much earlier.

Despite Goldwater's tub-thumping for bombing everything that moved in Vietnam, he made other comments suggesting that as president he might have tried to find a nonmilitary resolution. Criticizing Johnson's handling of the war, Goldwater said he would have sent Eisenhower to Vietnam with a group of experts to determine a solution,[20] hinting that he was ultimately after peace.

One certainty is that little of Johnson's legislative agenda would have survived. Despite strong Democratic House and Senate majorities, without a President Johnson to arm-twist, cajole, and threaten for votes, many of those initiatives would have died on the vine. How many Democrats would have risked supporting the Voting Rights Act without the president to give cover? Medicare and Medicaid would almost certainly not have been created given that Goldwater-advocate Ronald Reagan had been giving American Medical Association–funded speeches calling the system a totalitarian socialist takeover. Goldwater's antagonism to legislative and judicial remedies for racism might also have slowed or stopped the dismantling of Jim Crow.

How would a President Goldwater have reacted to the hippies? The protest movement's antiestablishment animus in the late 1960s had a bipartisan element: they despised Republican bigotry and insularity as much as they hated Democratic support for the Vietnam War. If Goldwater had never fully engaged in Vietnam, he might have also created a more united front between mainstream Democrats and progressives, which in turn might have made Republican victory in 1968 less assured. No President Nixon would mean no Watergate, a scandal which reverberated through 1970s domestic politics more than any other single event.

If Goldwater had won reelection in 1968, it would have cemented a new kind of Republican orthodoxy years before Reagan willed it into reality.

It could also have led to nuclear war.

———◇◇◇◇◇———

RONALD REAGAN
- vs. -
JIMMY CARTER

The beauty of Ronald Reagan's personality is that it does not concede the necessity for change and growth, does not concede error, does not concede hypocrisy.

—Garry Trudeau

The nine most terrifying words in the English language are: I'm from the government, and I'm here to help.

—Ronald Reagan

★ ★ ★ ★ ★ ★ ★

——— The Candidates ———

*President: Ronald Reagan
*Vice President: George H. W. Bush
Party: Republican
Popular / Electoral Votes: 43,901,812 / 489

President: Jimmy Carter
Vice President: Walter Mondale
Party: Democrat
Popular / Electoral Votes: 35,483,820 / 49

President: John Anderson
Vice President: Patrick Lucey
Party: Independent
Popular / Electoral Votes: 5,719,850 / 0

* = Winning candidates

WHY IT MATTERED

The 1970s in America at times felt like, as the old historian's cliché goes, just one damned thing after another. The chaos and defeatism clouding the end of the Vietnam War only ramped up with Watergate and the spirit-wilting series of American evils exposed by Congressional investigations. Shocks from inflation to fuel shortages chipped away at the nation's postwar sense of economic invulnerability. "White flight" from cities to mushrooming suburbs and fights over school integration kept racial tensions high. From 1965 to 1975, violent crime rates more than doubled. Sensationalist tabloid and television coverage of lurid stories like the Son of Sam murders made some of the population reluctant to leave the house.

American hegemony helped prevent major wars after 1945. But in the 1960s and '70s, coups and insurgencies—often fed by surrogates in the US–Soviet Cold War—rippled from South America through Africa and Asia. Terrorism flourished in Europe and the Middle East. Domestically, splinter factions of the anti-war Left, largely mainstreamed into the Democratic Party after Watergate, bombed hundreds of targets. While most attacks resulted in no casualties, they spread real terror as intended by groups like the Weather Underground, whose 1974 manifesto declared "Our intention is to disrupt the empire . . . to put pressure on the cracks."[1]

Near the end of the disrupted decade, the cracks were showing, and there was a dearth of leaders who could patch them.

The 1950s and '60s had presented a series of larger-than-life presidents like John F. Kennedy and Lyndon Johnson. Despite his remove and caution, Dwight Eisenhower carried himself with the gravitas and resolve appropriate for the general who led the invasion of Europe that toppled Hitler. Even the almost anti-telegenic Richard Nixon crafted an image as a daring leader willing to take bold moves, whether it was opening relations with China or establishing the EPA. His more criminal activities, from the Watergate scandal cover-up to secretly bombing Cambodia, may have only burnished his profile as a leader of action for his more dedicated supporters.

Compared to these men, the down-to-earth, incremental styles of the likes of Gerald Ford and Jimmy Carter looked pallid and uninspiring.

Slotted into the Nixon administration in 1973 to replace Spiro Agnew after he quit amid a bribery scandal, the understated and luckless Ford was as unlikely a president as Harry Truman three decades before. Uninspiring to conservatives, Ford narrowly eked out the 1976 Republican nomination. His Democratic opponent Carter also failed to fire up his party and narrowly won the presidency. He entered the White House as a smiling reformer, alight with moralistic enthusiasm and ready to tackle issues ranging from human rights to the environment. But the decade and its problems were far from over. Carter was in for a rough four years.

Meanwhile, the Republicans were actively seeking a new leader. The party's foreign-policy hawks were furious at what they saw as the post-Watergate hobbling of presidential power. At the same time, small-government ideologues and Christian fundamentalists had their eye out for the next Barry Goldwater.

After losing a close-fought nomination battle at the 1976 Republican convention, Ronald Reagan, the recent governor of California, gave a speech about writing a letter for a time capsule to be opened in one hundred years. Sounding more like the nominee than an also-ran, he imagined that, "if we failed, they probably won't get to read the letter at all because it spoke of individual freedom, and they won't be allowed to talk of that or read of it." The response to his oracular words and soaring cadences, which neatly stitched together Book of Revelations scaremongering with sunshine positivity, was explosive and nearly religious in its fervor.[2]

The Republicans had found their man. They just needed to wait four more years to vote for him.

RONALD REAGAN

Born in 1911 and raised in a series of small downstate Illinois towns, Ronald "Dutch" Reagan (the nickname came from his alcoholic father, who remarked that the newborn boy looked "like a fat little Dutchman"[3]) was graced with a strong jaw, a honied and mellifluous voice, an unbending optimism, the gift of gab, and a resolute drive to be a hero.

After knocking around in the Depression-era Midwest as a sports radio guy (he would read the news wires' play-by-play of Chicago Cubs games and reenact them for the audience), Reagan made it to California. There, his good looks and good-enough acting chops made him a solid lower-tier star who called himself "the Errol Flynn of the B-pictures."

Like most small-town Midwesterners who grew up during the Great Depression, Reagan was a rock-solid Democrat who voted for FDR four times, as he would frequently remind people later in life. But he reacted poorly to the activists and occasional communists in the Screen Actors Guild, which he led for several years.

In the 1950s, he made a hard turn to the right, even helping to establish the blacklist by testifying as a friendly witness before the House Un-American Activities Committee. Through the postwar years, his ideas kept tilting conservative, while his acting career dried up—though not before he co-starred with a rascally chimpanzee in 1951's *Bedtime for Bonzo*, which gave satirists reams of gags before Reagan got anywhere close to Washington.

Reagan switched to the Republican Party in 1962. His "A Time for Choosing" speech, televised in October 1964, quickly became legend. Meant as a last-minute boost for the flagging Barry Goldwater, it defined a vigorous new conservative ethos that rejected the Great Society and embraced a hard anti-Soviet line served as a call to arms. The speech failed to help Goldwater but planted the seed of a nascent conservative movement. Floored by Reagan's ability to connect, Eisenhower mentored and plugged him into the Republican Party infrastructure.[4]

Riding a wave of frustration with high taxes, while lambasting welfare recipients and ducking charges of extremism with self-deprecating humor, Reagan surprisingly won the governorship of California in 1966. After an unsuccessful 1968 presidential bid, he served a second term as governor before launching his second failed presidential run in 1976. All the while he courted right-wing media and conservative influencers who could help make sure the third time was the charm.

JIMMY CARTER

James "Jimmy" Carter was also an ambitious small-town kid with a great big smile. But there the similarities with Reagan ended. Born in 1924, Carter was raised in Plains, Georgia. An aggressive striver who embodied his parents' devout religiosity, Carter worked on the family farm, sold peanuts on the street, was named high school valedictorian, became a naval officer in 1946, and spent several years on submarines while also studying nuclear physics.

After his father died in 1953, Carter abandoned a promising Navy career and returned to Plains with his wife and children to run the family farm and store. Within a few years, the Carters turned the Golden Peanut Company into a multimillion-dollar business. He entered local politics with a passion for improving schooling and a staunch opposition to segregation, the latter of which drew antagonism from white neighbors. Despite entering the race just weeks before the election, he won a state senate seat in 1962. Losing his first gubernatorial run in 1966, Carter won in 1970 after four years of grinding campaigning.

As governor, Carter was as involved in the details of the job as Reagan was detached from his, reading every word of the hundreds of bills he needed to sign or veto.[5] Despite having worked with arch-segregationist Lester Maddox to win the election, once in office Carter pursued a strongly pro-civil rights agenda and trimmed the state's bloated bureaucracy.

The reaction to his 1976 presidential candidacy was neatly summed up by a headline in the *Atlanta Constitution*: "Jimmy Who Is Running for What!?" With a shoe-string budget but fierce dedication, he and his "Peanut Brigade" won a surprise victory in Iowa and quickly out-flanked better-known and deeper-pocketed Democratic rivals like Jerry Brown and Hubert Humphrey.[6]

Carter won the same kind of victory in the general election, running with an outsider's zeal and folksy warmth against a somewhat flummoxed Ford. With the help of a unified South thrilled to see one of their own in the White House for the first time in a century, and general dissatisfaction over Ford's pardon of Nixon, Carter won by just over a million votes. It was a stunning ascent, described by one former volunteer as "like discovering that the geeky kid with braces down the street had suddenly emerged as a Hollywood leading man."[7]

Four years later, of course, Carter would be running against an actual Hollywood leading man.

THE ELECTION

When asked by a reporter in the 1950s what was most likely to derail his administration's plans, British prime minister Harold Macmillan replied, "Events, dear boy, events." These are a few of the events that crashed onto President Carter's desk: rising inflation, high unemployment, a weak economy, an ongoing energy crisis, the Soviet invasion of Afghanistan, and a disastrous attempt to rescue the Americans held hostage after the

1979 Iranian Revolution. Despite Carter securing some impressive foreign-policy wins, including mediating a peace treaty between Israel and Egypt and signing the SALT II treaty with the Soviets to limit nuclear weapons, he was never able to get out from under the onslaught of negative events. This left him highly vulnerable to a challenge in 1980. As Ford had learned in 1976, incumbency was not a sure ticket to reelection.

Carter came into office with bold ideas about reforming the government, but not many plans for doing so. An energetic campaigner, in office he showed little appetite for the glad-handing and deal-making that greases the wheels of policy and influence. Because of that, and his tendency to go after popular pork barrel projects, Carter's relationship with Congress was hampered from the start, despite strong Democratic majorities in both chambers.

There was also his demeanor. Many reporters thought he was the smartest politician they had ever met. But he could also be somewhat insufferably arrogant and condescending.

Carter's strengths were often his weaknesses. Promising to level with the American people, he failed to appreciate that harsh truths go down better with a promise of a brighter future. He was an iconoclastic centrist who pursued left-wing ideals such as promoting human-rights causes abroad and alternative energy domestically, but also conservative policies on deregulation, deficit-cutting, and building up NATO to counter the Soviets.

What Carter could never do, though, was tie these zig-zagging positions into a coherent ideology or vision that could be communicated to a people anxious about America's apparently fading vitality. "Because Carter cannot explain what he is doing," wrote one of his former speechwriters in 1979, "he is an easy mark" for politicians like Reagan "who can speak with passion about the decline of American power."[8] Despite having what many confidants and even family members suggested was a hollow center beneath the shiny façade, Reagan had no problem speaking with passion.

Reagan announced his candidacy in November 1979, just two months before the Iowa caucuses. Although he lost Iowa to former CIA director George H. W. Bush and faced concern over his age, he won the nomination with relative ease and named Bush his running mate. Brushing aside more moderate candidates like Illinois' John Anderson—who launched a surprisingly potent third-party bid—Reagan blithely claimed he could balance the budget while lowering taxes and increasing military spending.

Carter's nomination was more of a fight. Criticized as an ineffectual centrist by the party's left wing and facing low approval ratings, he had to fight off a challenge by Ted Kennedy, possibly the party's biggest star. "I'll whip his ass," the intensely competitive Carter told a group of Congressmen,[9] again rousing himself more for the fight than for what followed. He won the nomination, thanks to Kennedy's flubbing a question about why he wanted to be president and residual concern over Kennedy's role in Mary Jo Kopechne's drowning in 1969. But the rapturous reaction at the convention to Kennedy's speech, complete with chants of "We want Ted,"[10] left the nominee looking like an afterthought.

Reagan was leading in the summer of 1980 but hit a few rough patches on the campaign trail. He was criticized for telling a crowd of born-again Christians that creationism should be taught in schools and voicing support for "state's rights" (still code for segregation) at a Mississippi fair near where civil rights workers had been murdered in 1964.

Blowing past controversies with an aw-shucks grin and a breezy declaration that Happy Days Are Here Again, the apple-cheeked Reagan seemed too nice to be the scary extremist that Carter's campaign kept warning about. Reagan was canny, photogenic, always ready with a quip or inspirational story (some of which may even have been true), and better equipped than any Republican in decades for smuggling far-right ideas into the mainstream.

Meanwhile Carter flailed. In the face of Reagan's gauzy and fantastical promises, the truth-telling Carter looked like a dour scold. By 1980, the Democratic coalition of minorities and progressive whites had frayed. Without a Kennedy or a Johnson to rally the troops, Democrats seemed more driven by nostalgia for the great struggles of the 1960s (civil rights, the Great Society, the Vietnam War) than energized to fight the fights of the 1970s. The War on Poverty was a staggering accomplishment—leveraging Medicare, Medicaid, Head Start, Legal Services, Upward Bound, and other programs to pull millions out of poverty and dramatically expand access to health care, education, and legal representation. But Democrats declined to take credit, leaving room for Republicans to seed doubt and racially coded anger about "welfare queens" and "government waste."

While Carter wanted to launch new government programs, Reagan promised to have government do less. This mantra, which played like his old mentor Goldwater with the zanier libertarian edges sanded off, had not yet become Republican gospel. It played effectively into the anti-institutional antagonism that had started on the left in the 1960s. By the 1970s, it fully pervaded the mainstream. Americans' trust in the federal government peaked at 77 percent in 1964. By the election of 1980, it plummeted to under 30 percent.[11]

Reagan's cleverly targeted messaging to specific constituencies was matched by vaguer commitments on the national stage. It worked well enough for his post-Goldwater coalition of social conservatives, defense hawks, unreconstructed racists, anti-tax libertarians, business leaders, and less ideological types looking for a strong leader. Although sixty-nine (older than any other elected president), he radiated vigor. Carter, unable to fix the dreary economy and having performed poorly in the debate, looked especially ineffectual when the first anniversary of the Iran hostage crisis landed on Election Day with no end in sight.

It was a landslide for Reagan, who won 44 states. Republicans swept the South, West, and Midwest, furthering the party's inroads into formerly Democratic white, ethnic, union, and Catholic households.

Reagan's campaign slogan said, "Let's Make America Great Again." Whether or not he followed through on that pledge is an open question.

THE MALAISE SPEECH

—◇◇◇◇◇—

There is likely no better symbol of the chasm separating Carter and Reagan in style and substance than Carter's "Crisis of Confidence" speech televised on July 15, 1979. Carter told Americans that the "erosion of our confidence in the future" was a threat to social comity despite the nation's "unmatched economic power and military might." Framing energy conservation as a patriotic mobilization to cut dependence on foreign oil, he announced bold initiatives including a $10 billion public transportation plan and Congressional authorization for "gasoline rationing." He said it would not be easy, but that there "is simply no way to avoid sacrifice." Later mocked as the "Malaise Speech" (though he never used that word), it was often later referred to as a crucial misstep that helped kill Carter's reelection bid. That was both true and not true. The president's approval ratings actually jumped afterward, and 61 percent of the public said the speech gave them confidence.[12] However, his doleful tone resonated more in the long-term than the optimism of his message. Future presidents of both parties took note and avoided both ambitious environmental plans and requests for sacrifice from the American people.

THE AFTERMATH

In a serendipitous moment that could have been scripted for one of Reagan's lesser B-movies, on the day of his inauguration, a plane took off from Tehran with the remaining hostages. This ended their 14-month ordeal and neatly turned Carter's political albatross into a boost for Reagan even as he delivered his address calling for "an era of national renewal." (Some Republicans later claimed Iran turned over the hostages because the tough-talking new president scared them. In fact, it followed months of negotiations by Carter's team, including the transfer of billions of dollars in frozen assets and the Iranians' reluctance to restart talks with a new administration.)

Two months into his administration, Reagan was shot and wounded by a mentally ill man after a speech in Washington. Reagan survived and found time during his recovery to phone in a few gags to the White House Correspondents' Dinner. But the experience left him more shaken than he would admit and resulted in a more fervent embrace of his evangelical faith.

A top priority for the new administration was the enactment of "Reaganomics." Throughout the campaign, Reagan had promised to balance the budget by cutting taxes, shrinking government, and raising military spending. During the campaign, Bush derisively referred to this widely and repeatedly debunked exercise in magical thinking as "voodoo economics." But the public was ready to believe in the impossible. So, too, were conservatives who embraced the theories promised by economists Milton Friedman and Arthur Laffer, who argued that lowering taxes and cutting regulations would incentivize productivity and generate greater revenue.

The first part of the administration's sweeping redirection of government priorities included the largest tax and spending cuts in history. The Economic Recovery Tax Act dramatically reduced income taxes. While about half of those cuts were later rolled back,[13] the Act sent a strong signal. Reagan followed that up by slashing billions in spending, mostly from programs helping the poor.[14] As working families lost aid and mental institutions shut down (swelling the homeless population), deficits exploded. Cannily, Reagan left intact FDR's New Deal programs that provided universal help, like Social Security, while going after Great Society programs designed to assist select groups. "I'm trying to undo the 'Great Society'," he wrote in his diary. "It was LBJ's war on poverty that led to our present mess."[15]

Reagan's staff appeared more organized and driven than Carter's. Despite having to extensively wrangle with the Democratic House, they had a Republican-led Senate, the first since 1952, to work with. Another great contrast with the micromanaging Carter was the new president's management style, honed during his days as governor. Reagan enthusiastically delegated responsibility for working out the details of his grand plans. The former actor specialized in the messaging, pageantry, and showmanship needed to sell the transformative agenda.

By 1983, the economy had significantly strengthened and national morale had improved. The stock market was booming and more obvious signs of concern, like long gas lines, had disappeared. Economists disagree over whether this was due to Reagan's tax cuts or several years of Carter-appointed Fed Chairman Paul Volcker's anti-inflationary measures. But while things were great on the penthouse level, economic conditions for the middle class barely improved and the poor were in many cases worse off.

On the foreign policy side, Reagan's moves were just as dramatic. Convinced that détente was little more than appeasement, the administration's hardline Cold Warriors wanted to take the fight to the USSR, or what Reagan called the "Evil Empire," without starting an actual war. The Pentagon's budget exploded. Covert aid flowed to mujahideen fighting the Soviet army occupying Afghanistan and to Contra rebels battling Soviet-backed Sandinistas in Nicaragua. Reagan's aggressive brinksmanship—deploying more missiles to Europe, criticizing arms control treaties, announcing an antagonizing missile-defense system more fantasy than reality—caused greater panic about a nuclear exchange than had been seen since the 1962 Cuban Missile Crisis. Domestic resistance resulted in Congressional action blocking aid to the Contras, an ineffectual band better at human rights abuses than victories, and limiting administration plans to expand the nuclear arsenal.[16]

Still, when Carter's vice president Walter Mondale stepped up to challenge Reagan in 1984, there was little indication Reagan had much to fear. It was already clear he could regularly engage in contradictions that would have ended the careers of lesser politicians (e.g., raising taxes to fund Medicare, the supposed socialist nightmare he once said would destroy America[17]). Democratic Colorado congresswoman Pat Schroeder observed that Reagan "has been perfecting the Teflon-coated presidency. He sees to it that nothing sticks to him."[18]

At his convention, Reagan rhapsodized vaguely about how "every opportunity . . . is still golden in this land," while Mondale tried to emulate Carter and level with people at the Democratic convention: "Taxes will go up. And anyone who says they won't is not telling the truth to the American people." By then, voters were even less interested in truth-telling than they had been in 1980. Reagan won 49 of 50 states and even made a late campaign visit to Minnesota to try and make it a clean sweep.

Democrats suffered a devastating loss in 1984. Mondale did very well in several larger cities.[19] But it was less a vote for him than a vote of disgust for Reagan's militarism, neglect of the poor, and silence on the growing HIV/AIDS crisis. For the Republicans, 1984 was the solidifying victory they had been seeking for twenty years.

Besides decisively reclaiming the South from the Democrats and establishing strong bases of support throughout the West and Midwest, this win in 1984 also brought moderate Republicans back into the fold. As Reagan's ideas became mainstream conservative ideas, he appeared less a radical and more the avuncular living saint that the party apparatus had already begun to canonize.

Reagan's second-term foreign policy victories, particularly the summits with Soviet leader Mikhail Gorbachev, did not amount to much in terms of actual arms limitations, but they helped reduce the belligerence of his first term. Domestically, his second-term record was tattered. Corruption at the EPA, kickbacks at the Pentagon, and illegal lobbying by the president's advisors did not implicate Reagan directly, but they showed how anti-regulatory fervor can lead to lax ethical standards.[20] His administration's extreme anti-Communism resulted in the illegal arms smuggling scheme known as Iran-Contra. But despite all the investigations and televised hearings, the Teflon president emerged mostly unscathed.

Shortly after Reagan left office, the Berlin Wall fell, the Soviet era came to an end, and Western capitalist democracy emerged triumphant after the great struggles of the twentieth century. The Republicans gladly took credit, secure in the knowledge that the Reagan presidency had made them the dominant force in American politics.

WHAT IF...?

Barring an unforeseen October Surprise, there is little that could have won Carter the presidency in 1980. But if the initially favored Ted Kennedy had hung on to more supporters and managed an upset at the convention, then Reagan may have at least had a serious challenger.

Although he eventually rehabilitated himself as an expert architect of legislation, the scandal-scarred Kennedy would have had a hard time keeping media attention

REAGAN AND THE UNIONS

———⊶∞⊷———

Reagan had campaigned as a proud union man. But his decision in August 1981 to replace most of the 13,000 striking members of the Professional Air Traffic Controllers Organization (PATCO) and decertify their union set a precedent for companies who had not previously dared to replace striking workers. Reagan's forceful action, and his administration's anti-union zeal, further eroded the power of American labor, which had been in decline since deindustrialization started in the 1970s. But while in keeping with Reagan's fashionable free-market ideology, it was a stark turnabout for the only president who had himself been a union member. Two decades earlier, he even led a daring, skillfully negotiated Screen Actors Guild strike that pried industry-changing concessions, such as residual payments and health and pension benefits, from the movie studios. Perhaps if Reagan had come up as an air traffic controller, things would have gone better for PATCO.

off of his drinking and womanizing and focused on his presidency. Based on his time in the Senate, though, a Ted Kennedy presidency would have leveraged his considerable dealmaking skills to muscle through more significant bills on at least some of his signature policies than Democrats had managed since the 1960s. If Kennedy had successfully implemented even a rudimentary national health insurance system in the 1980s, the entire arc of

American politics would have shifted, likely giving Democrats room to focus on other programs and building up the Great Society that Reagan wanted to scrap.

Without the "Reagan Revolution" kicking off decades of deregulation and economic policies favoring the wealthy, the growth of inequality and diminishment of the middle class may not have happened as quickly. As a more charismatic Democrat than Carter or Mondale, Kennedy could have sold a more liberal message that the country might have bought, especially after the economy started improving.

In terms of foreign policy, it is easier to say what President Ted Kennedy would *not* have done. Broadly opposed to military adventurism, he would almost certainly not have increased the military budget or launched easy-to-win symbolic scraps like the invasion of Grenada or bombing of Libya. He would not have given brutal dictators like Chile's Augusto Pinochet a pass because they were anti-communist, nor funded a host of wars in developing nations. By not providing money and arms to Afghanistan, Kennedy would have let the Soviet occupation drag on longer but with the benefit of not providing arsenals, training, and legitimacy to the America-hating fighters who later formed al-Qaeda. If Kennedy had won reelection, he would not have let Reagan's pipe dream missile defense program SDI ("Star Wars") keep him from making the world-changing arms-control agreement that Gorbachev wanted.

Republicans' deregulatory and tax-cutting fervor would not have gone away without a President Reagan.

The network of conservative activists and think tanks funded by billionaires like Richard Mellon Scaife, the Coors family, and the Koch brothers were highly committed, disciplined, skilled at propaganda, and patient. In other words, the opposite of the fractious, ill-defined Democratic Party of the 1970s and '80s. But a President Kennedy could have reinvigorated the party. A Reagan defeat could have been viewed as a repudiation of his ideals, leaving small-government conservatives to try their luck again, only with a far less attractive candidate.

And in politics, a Ronald Reagan does not come around that often.

2008

BARACK OBAMA
- VS. -
JOHN MCCAIN

At the heart of Obama's narrative was a belief that progress, in the larger scheme of things, was inevitable.

—George Packer

There's a slight madness to thinking you should be the leader of the free world.

—Barack Obama

THE CANDIDATES

*President: Barack Obama
*Vice President: Joe Biden
Party: Democratic
Popular / Electoral Votes: 69,456,897 / 365

President: John McCain
Vice President: Sarah Palin
Party: Republican
Popular / Electoral Votes: 59,934,814 / 173

* = Winning candidates

WHY IT MATTERED

The end of the Cold War left America the world's sole superpower. For the first time in nearly half a century, America was not locked in a nuclear-armed standoff. American presidents had often been called the "Leader of the Free World." With the collapse of the Soviet Union and former Warsaw Pact countries transitioning to democracy, that description suddenly seemed far more open-ended. Without a perpetual enemy abroad, America turned inward again. Only it was still in possession of a nuclear arsenal and a world-spanning military machine that it was in no hurry to give up.

Immediately following Reagan, presidential contests cycled more around style, signaling, and media narratives than sharp policy differences. The parties seemed divided more over cultural issues like gay marriage and abortion than economics or foreign policy. There were still great geographical divides between the parties. But elections came to be even more about proxy fights for longstanding grudges: urban versus rural, religious versus secular, "elites" versus "real America."

With the Soviet Union and Jim Crow gone, despite the persistence of totalitarianism abroad and racism at home, many Americans thought there were no more big fights left. Echoing the laissez-faire consensus of the pre–Teddy Roosevelt years, the 1990s saw Democrats and Republicans arguing nuances on taxation while at a higher level often agreeing on cutting social welfare spending, packing prisons through harsher sentencing laws, and loosening New Deal–era financial regulations to open up the economy. Both parties also agreed on freeing trade, with Democrats brushing aside the concerns of labor to pass the North American Free Trade Agreement (NAFTA). Due partially to this consensus, the 1990s saw the rise of third-party candidates like consumer advocate Ralph Nader and quirky Texas billionaire Ross Perot who argued that Republicans and Democrats were two sides of the same coin.

Beating Reagan's patrician successor George H. W. Bush in 1992 with disarming warmth and a message of "it's the economy, stupid," Arkansas governor Bill Clinton did what Democrats had failed to do since the 1960s: Capture the hearts and minds of middle-class suburban voters.[1] But despite Democratic House and Senate majorities, his signature policies such as universal health care and ending the ban on gays in the military went down in defeat. Clinton's "triangulation" tactic poached conservative causes like welfare reform and harsher criminal sentencing that saw short-term tactical gains, shifted the party dramatically to the center-right, and ultimately made nobody happy. He disappointed liberals who were mostly shut out of party leadership and enraged conservatives who still saw Clinton as a draft-dodging hippie libertine who had cut his hair and put on a tie.

Conservatives were mobilized by daily culture-war outrage delivered by talk-radio shouters. Caught off-guard by the groundswell, Democrats lost the House and Senate in 1994. Led by Georgia congressman Newt Gingrich, the 1990s Republican wave brought back a style of ferocious no-quarter legislative combat that hadn't been seen since the pre–Civil War years but would prove to be the new normal.

Things were no better for Clinton after his 1996 reelection. House Republicans voted in 1998 to impeach Clinton after being spurred by scandals ranging from real (Clinton's affair with an intern) to fantasy (claims the Clintons had their friend Vincent Foster murdered after his suicide in 1993). The second presidential impeachment trial in history ended in Clinton's acquittal by the Senate. But despite Clinton's high approval, the taint of scandal kept him from campaigning in 2000 with his vice president, the less politically adept Al Gore.

Gore fought an often content-free campaign against Texas governor George W. Bush, a sunny evangelical who appeared more down-to-earth than Gore even though both were silver-spoon Ivy Leaguers. Gore beat Bush by over a half-million votes, but the Electoral College was unsettled due to vote-counting irregularities in Florida. The Supreme Court's five Republican appointees ruled against Gore in stopping the weeks-long recount. The second President Bush entered the White House under a cloud of questions about his legitimacy. There was a new national debate about the anti-democratic nature of the Electoral College, which had now elected four presidents who lost the popular vote. Once again, the debate went nowhere.

After the September 11, 2001, terror attacks by the Islamic extremist network al-Qaeda, the first assault on American soil since Pearl Harbor, the nation faced an unfamiliar conundrum: For once, the question was not whether to retaliate but who to retaliate against. "We are At War now," wrote Hunter S. Thompson on September 12. "We will stay At War with that mysterious Enemy for the rest of our lives."[2] What came to be known as the "War on Terror"—murky, ill-defined, poorly planned, secretive, sometimes lawless, borderless, and defying conventional stratagems or methods of closure—occupied Bush's two terms and rumbled on through the presidencies that followed, seemingly without end and eventually ignored by most Americans on the home front. Legislation like the Patriot Act curtailed individual freedoms while human-rights abuses by the CIA and military damaged America's international reputation nearly as much as the Vietnam War's My Lai massacre.

WAR ON TERROR

—◦◦◦◦—

Bush's "War on Terror" was actually three wars. First was the invasion of Afghanistan in late 2001, a decisive but shallow victory that quickly toppled the Taliban who then launched a fierce guerrilla war that American and allied forces were unable to stamp out. The second war was Iraq, which the U.S. invaded in March 2003 after an effort by the White House to falsely link Iraqi dictator Saddam Hussein to al-Qaeda. America again won the conventional war in a flash, but a brutal insurgency resisted American attempts to quell it. The third war was a diffuse international conflict in which American covert operatives assassinated suspected members of the terrorist cells blinking into existence across Africa, the Middle East, and Asia. Following a brief interregnum after the Cold War, the post-9/11 era presented America and its leaders with a new perpetual enemy in fanatic Islamic terrorism, just as ideologically driven as communism but stateless this time and forever shifting.

The president who followed Bush would inherit the War on Terror's excesses and costs, as well as a question about what kind of world leader America would be (or indeed if it should be a world leader at all).

BARACK OBAMA

The 2008 Democratic candidate was so new to national politics that four years earlier most of the country had never heard of him. Decades after Reagan made his name giving a speech for a losing candidate, Barack Obama did the same.

Still failing to capture the middle of the electorate with mushy messaging and cowed by the threat of being called unpatriotic in wartime, in 2004 the Democrats put up Senator John Kerry, another tall, bright, and well-meaning but arrogant stiff who was an easy target for Bush's relaxed charm. At the convention, Obama thrilled the crowd with a more electrifying version of his stump speech attacking the "negative ad peddlers" who sliced the country into demographics and tried to make them fight: "[T]here's not a liberal America and a conservative America; there's the *United States* of America." Depleted by three years of the War on Terror and its abuses and executive overreach, Democrats received the speech like water in the Sahara.

A professorial presence whose fulsome emotional rhetoric contrasted with his dry wit, Obama had a more varied upbringing than any previous presidential candidate. Raised in Hawaii by his white Kansan mother after a stint living in Indonesia and never really knowing his black Kenyan father, Obama spent much of his young life searching for identity. After college, he took a low-paying community organizer job in Chicago. Living and working in the city's black neighborhoods made him feel rooted for the first time. He left to earn a law degree at Harvard, excelling as a peacemaker between rival political factions at the *Harvard Law Review*, where he was the first black president. Back in Chicago after law school, he served in the state senate before making a surprise run for the U.S. Senate.

A disciplined and calculated man who took nothing for granted, Obama also had an aura of serendipity about him. In the spring of 2004, after Obama had won the Democratic nomination, a sex scandal forced out Republican nominee Jack Ryan. Scrambling for a last-minute replacement, the party tapped Alan Keyes, a Catholic zealot radio host who did not live in Illinois and had been unsuccessfully running for office since the late 1980s. Obama realized he had just been handed the election. "You are the luckiest bastard in the world," his campaign manager told him.[3]

The soon-to-be senator did not disagree. It was likely part of the reason that two years later, after prudently keeping his head down in the Senate, he decided to take a shot at becoming America's first black president.

JOHN MCCAIN

A political pundit cliché goes: "Democrats fall in love; Republicans fall in line." Given the giddy excitement that accrued around Obama, the first part of that line was certainly true in 2008, but not so much the second. John McCain was not a politician who fell in line, particularly when it came to the increasingly ideological homogeneity of the Republican party after the Reagan Revolution.

Born into a military family, McCain had large shoes to fill: his grandfather was a World War II naval commander, his father commanded all armed forces in the Pacific during the Vietnam War, and one ancestor served as an aide to George Washington. A hot-tempered student with lousy grades, McCain barely graduated from the Naval Academy. Coming into his own as a Navy pilot, he flew bombing missions over North Vietnam until being shot down in 1967. Heavily injured, he was imprisoned and tortured at the "Hanoi Hilton" for five and a half years, refusing to accept his jailors' offers of early release in order to keep them from scoring propaganda points.

Back home, working as Navy liaison to the Senate, McCain developed a taste for politics and a network of friendships and mentors. After two terms as an Arizona congressman, he was elected in 1986 to a U.S. Senate seat he held for the rest of his life. A national-security Republican with a self-professed "maverick" streak, he raised his profile by sometimes breaking with his party.

During McCain's White House run in 2000, his free-wheeling "Straight Talk Express" made him a favorite of reporters. But his breaking rank (i.e., calling Bush-championing evangelicals like Jerry Falwell "agents of intolerance") caused agitation with lockstep conservatives. After the racist smear offensive in South Carolina about McCain's adopted Bangladeshi daughter was linked to the Bush campaign[4]—like his father's campaign's character assassination of Michael Dukakis in 1988, W. preferred high rhetoric and gutter-level tactics—McCain likely never forgave his rival. But ever the loyal soldier, he gave his support after Bush won the nomination. Then he went back to being a senator, one of the increasingly rare Republicans in the chamber who would work with Democrats. He was close friends with Ted Kennedy. On an overseas trip in 2004, he challenged the Democratic senator from New York to a vodka shot drinking contest. Hillary Clinton obliged.

By 2008, McCain was ready for another shot at the presidency.

THE ELECTION

Despite its many dramas, 2008 was the sort of campaign that many political reporters hate covering. Both candidates had their quirks and distinctive characters. But their resolute character and lack of scandal left an ever-more hyperbolic media with nothing titillating to write about. Behind the rhetoric were two decent, whip-smart, mold-breaking candidates who had vociferous disagreements but were driven by a rock-solid faith in the democratic experiment and the American people. Despite both men's best intentions, it was destined to be another bruising electoral rumble as an increasingly polarized electorate used politics as proxy combat while the largest financial crisis since the Great Depression was darkening the horizon.

After announcing his candidacy in early 2007, Obama was not favored to win the Democratic nomination. The presumptive nominee was Hillary Clinton. While she was a formidable opponent, Obama's impressive grassroots organizing, staunch Iraq War opposition, and loosely stated theme of change beat out Clinton's political expertise gambit. A third candidate, the progressive former North Carolina senator John Edwards, dropped out relatively early.

McCain declared his candidacy on David Letterman's talk show in early 2007. After a rough start, he shifted to a ground-up campaign focused on town halls and convincing Republicans that his previous heresies—supporting immigration reform, criticizing tax cuts, fighting the Bush administration's torture of detainees—were a thing of the past. It never fully worked. He secured the nomination, partially due to weak rivals like Arkansas governor Mike Huckabee and former Massachusetts governor Mitt Romney who represented, respectively, the party's rural, evangelical and executive-suite factions. But Republicans remained uninspired by McCain, except for his last-minute vice-presidential selection of Alaska's little-known governor, Sarah Palin, a brassy born-again Christian whose love of God, guns, and one-liners thrilled crowds more than the man at the top of the ticket.

Obama attracted a high degree of excitement from his party despite critiques from centrists like Bill Clinton. Obama later quelled some concerns about his outsider status by choosing an exceptionally establishment running mate, his senatorial colleague Joe Biden. Obama's thoughtful, restrained, almost technocratic manner provided a sharp contrast for those frustrated by the Bush administration's overheated "Axis of Evil" rhetoric and poor governing record.

But Obama's campaign was put on the defensive by a deluge of conservative media outrage that outpaced even the previous decade's hatred of Bill Clinton. The bookish lawyer who loved quoting Protestant theologian Reinhold Niebuhr was accused of being secretly a socialist, gay, Muslim, terrorist sympathizing, Black Panther–esque America-hating radical, or some combination thereof. In a wrinkle worthy of the most vituperative nineteenth-century partisan journalism, even the veracity of Obama's birth certificate was questioned.

The conspiratorial panic was even faced by Obama's rival. McCain was booed by his own supporters at a Minnesota rally after telling them there was no reason to be "scared" of an Obama presidency. After a woman said, "I can't trust Obama . . . he's an Arab," McCain forcefully shut her down. "No, ma'am. He's a decent family man [and] citizen that I just happen to have disagreements with on fundamental issues."[5] McCain's character-revealing pushback against racist fear-mongering garnered him accolades, but mostly from those who would never vote for him. The party's anxious, angry heart was not with the war hero but rather the moose-hunting governor and self-professed "prayer warrior."[6]

It was not enough. The cratering economy, exhaustion with endless wars, and a lack of clarity about the nation's direction made the electorate more receptive to a dramatic, optimistic change in style and philosophy. Obama bested McCain handily in the popular vote, 53 percent to 46 percent. Showing that, in the end, Republicans would still fall in line, roughly the same number came out to vote for McCain as had for Bush in 2004. Promising a break from the Bush legacy that McCain looked likely to continue, Obama won by increasing overall turnout, particularly among young and black voters. Later analysis also suggested that Palin's extreme religious conservatism and inexperience pushed a block of voters off the fence toward Obama.[7]

Much of McCain's concession speech was devoted to praising his rival's character and historic accomplishment. Reminding people of the "outrage" Teddy Roosevelt received after inviting Booker T. Washington to the White House, McCain said America was now far removed from "the cruel and prideful bigotry of that time" and that he hoped there was "no reason now for any American to fail to cherish their citizenship in this, the greatest nation on Earth."

THE AFTERMATH

Despite his oratorical gifts and historic status, once Obama entered the Oval Office, he governed as more of an incrementalist, or a utilitarian reformer preferring practical wins to more symbolic risk. That philosophy was criticized by progressive Democrats as too easily compromising to put "points on the board."[8] Already caricatured as a revolutionary leftist, he was cautious not to appear radical. Obama's refusal to be pressured into short-sighted symbolic action was part of his fundamental optimism. That, along with his success collaborating with Republicans in Illinois,[9] likely blinded him to the political cost Washington Republicans would pay for working with him.

Previous presidents had room to operate with Congress. Democrats controlled the House for decades after FDR but were limited due to their conservative Southern members joining forces with Republicans. Moderate Rockefeller Republicans crossed party lines, too. But after the 1960s, ideologically similar Americans began geographically clustering. Nearly half the votes in the 2008 election came from "landslide" counties that went for their candidate by at least 20 percentage points; in 1976, only about a quarter of voters lived in landside counties.[10] This "Big Sort" shrank the number of competitive electoral districts, reduced politicians' ability to vote across party lines without repercussions, and turned conservative Democrats and liberal Republicans into endangered species.

President Obama's agenda ran straight into this buzz saw. Like many Democrats, he appeared not yet to understand the extent to which right-wing talk radio and Fox News had become the conservative movement's driving force, able to direct a blowtorch of fury against any Republicans who strayed. The din of criticism had become so extreme that in January 2009, Bush—believing the only way to save the faltering economy was for the country to rally around the new president, even if he was a rival—invited conservative talk-radio hosts to the White House to ask a favor: "Go easy on the new guy."[11] But Obama would soon have to face an entirely new phenomenon.

Ostensibly, the Tea Party was a reaction to the financial crisis. With the economy in free fall by February 2009,

THE FIRST BLACK PRESIDENT

———◇◇◇◇———

Although the historical significance must have weighed on Obama, he worked not to let it show. A student of history and literature, not to mention a politically astute person with eyes open to the country's racial ugliness, he knew that a democracy needed to show that progress was possible and not (per Langston Hughes) "a dream deferred." No previous black Democratic candidate—political veterans like Shirley Chisholm (1972), Jesse Jackson (1984), and Carol Moseley Braun (2004)—advanced far enough in the primaries to where the possibility of their becoming president had ever quite resonated. Before Obama, the potential for a black president was rarely seriously entertained. More often the idea was used as a vehicle for fish-out-of-water comedy, accompanied by concern that they would be assassinated or dismissed outright as impossible in a country with such systemic racism. But Obama, four years old when Congress finally protected the right of black Americans like himself to vote, succeeded in part through making his candidacy less a vehicle for political ideas than a transcendent symbol of progress and healing. The self-described "skinny kid with a funny name" made a vote for the first black president not just a mark on a ballot but a statement of confidence in the promise of America.

the Obama administration enacted a large-scale stimulus program that likely kept the Great Recession from turning into a depression. This effort was hampered by poor messaging, tactical mistakes, and a lack of visible improvements like infrastructure that could have shown the public where the hundreds of billions of dollars were going. Only three GOP Senators and no GOP House members voted for it. Then, Revolutionary War–themed protests (complete with tricornered hats, powdered wigs, and "Don't Tread on Me" flags) expressed outrage over the massive outlays.

Starting as a grassroots uprising, the Tea Party grew into the next reactionary Republican insurgency, well-funded by right-wing think tanks and business lobbies using the movement's loose libertarianism as cover for their tax- and regulation-cutting agendas.[12] Quickly taking up the culture war, with Palin as a new Phyllis Schlafly, the Tea Party targeted "un-American coastal elites" and equated liberal federalism with dictatorial socialism. With surprising speed, a movement that started out protesting taxpayer bailouts of billionaires and "too big to fail" banks switched to attacking not just government regulations, including the kind that could have stopped the 2008 crash,[13] but nearly *all* large government programs.

In early 2010, the Obama administration partnered with a Democratic-led Congress to pass a massive expansion of health insurance access called the Affordable Care Act (ACA) and the Dodd-Frank Wall Street Reform and Consumer Protection Act. Later that year, supercharged by a wave of Tea Party–allied newcomers (and helped along by an under-the-radar Republican campaign to sweep up state legislatures and control redistricting before the census), Republicans retook the House in the biggest midterm swing since 1938.

Obama easily overtook a somewhat hapless Mitt Romney to win reelection in 2012, but Congressional resistance was so fierce that debate over spending resulted in a sixteen-day government shutdown. By the end of Obama's second term, many of his policies were being enacted through executive orders, not legislation.

Domestic debates raged over the ACA, Dodd-Frank, and the 2015 Supreme Court ruling legalizing same-sex marriage. But as had been the case since Roosevelt and Johnson, the Democrats proved largely ineffective at communicating accomplishments to the electorate. Though the Reagan–Clinton-era free-market consensus started unraveling after the Great Recession, little was done to combat the income inequality, which, by Obama's second term, had reached levels not seen since 1928.[14]

Also in Obama's second term, a string of killings of unarmed black men by police resulted in widespread outrage and protests. Anti-police rhetoric reached a crescendo not seen since the late 1960s. While awareness of systemic racism grew widely, so did the tenor of resistance from those who refused to acknowledge it. Due to this impasse, the number of Americans who thought white-black relations were good dropped dramatically.[15] The number of white supremacist hate groups began proliferating in 2015.[16] That year, a twenty-one-year-old

Confederate sympathizer wanting to start a "race war" walked into a historic black church in Charleston, South Carolina, and killed nine worshippers.

Obama's party looked to him for leadership and healing during those increasing eruptions of domestic hate. But his foreign policy was relatively unscrutinized by the party, which became less concerned about executive overreach once a Democrat was in the White House. Campaigning as an idealist, he struck a more pragmatic stance in office. In a 2002 anti-war speech, he had decried the invasion of Iraq while noting that he was no pacifist, just against "a dumb war." As president, he kept much of the existing lower-profile counterinsurgency strategy (assassinations, drone strikes) in place while avoiding the Bush era's interventionist hubris, now unpopular with both parties. For the sake of clarity to his staff, Obama often boiled his thinking down to a simple rule: "Don't do stupid shit."[17] It was a practical approach, but its specificity and seeming lack of vision left many wondering what Obama thought America's place in the world should be.

By the end of Obama's administration, entropy was gnawing at what was left of George H. W. Bush's "New World Order." A newly expansionist Russia annexed Crimea and agitated for civil war in Ukraine. China established bases in the South China Sea and claimed international waters as its own. The newer Islamic extremist group ISIS conquered a wide swath of Iraq and Syria. The Russia-backed Syrian government committed mass atrocities against its people. Except for providing air

support to the fight against ISIS, the Obama administration mostly stayed out of these fracases, worried that
human-rights concerns or Kissinger-esque realpolitik
could immerse America in new quagmires.

Many Republicans, despite their frustration with the
Bush administration's overreach and incompetence, began
to miss the cowboy swagger of those years as compared
with Obama's caution. Foreign policy veterans of both
parties worried that the apparent withdrawal of America
from the world scene would lead to greater chaos.

WHAT IF...?

McCain's selection of Palin undermined his case for
returning effective leadership to the White House. But
his Republican bona fides would have been more jeop-
ardized if he had gone with his first choice: independent
former Democrat Joe Lieberman. Other Republican
frontrunners would not have fared better. Romney's
2012 performance showed his inability to garner support from soon-to-be Tea Party populists. Huckabee's
genial, joking nature might have helped win over non-
evangelical Republicans but it's doubtful it would have
been enough to overcome Obama.

However, if John Edwards had not abandoned his
candidacy so early, his more economically progressive and
actively reformist message could have resonated enough
for him to win the nomination. An Edwards presidency
would still have caused a Tea Party–like response, especially given that he may have been far more activist than

Obama. At the same time, the eventual revelation of the married Edwards' affair would likely have felt like Clinton redux—another smiley Southerner caught in flagrante delicto. This could potentially have put the Republicans in a better position for 2012.

Without the reality of a President Obama to run against, it is also possible that the 2016 Republican candidate may never have bestirred himself to descend from his gold-covered tower to lead the next revolt.

———◦◦×◦◦———

★ 2016 ★

DONALD TRUMP
– VS. –
HILLARY CLINTON

Mastery of TV was now not just a political tool but a presidential qualification in itself. Even Reagan had to become governor of California first.

—James Poniewozik

No puppet. No puppet. You're the puppet!

—Donald Trump

THE CANDIDATES

*President: Donald Trump
*Vice President: Mike Pence
Party: Republican
Popular / Electoral Votes: 62,980,160 / 304

President: Hillary Clinton
Vice President: Tim Kaine
Party: Democrat
Popular / Electoral Votes: 65,845,063 / 227

* = Winning candidates

WHY IT MATTERED

The end of the modern Republican Party might have happened not in a voting booth or meeting of party elders, but at the 2011 White House Correspondents' Association Dinner. That night, President Barack Obama and TV comic Seth Myers took several pot-shots at Donald Trump, seething in the audience. Some writers later promulgated a theory that was not entirely likely, yet impossible to disprove, and containing just enough dark irony to perfectly match the stew of conspiracy and rage that typified American politics in the second decade of the new millennium.

Trump had been talking about running for president for so long it seemed like just another thing he always said. But earlier in 2011, Trump had started promoting the "birther" falsehood about Obama's non-U.S. citizenship, as unkillable a conspiracy theory as NASA faking the moon landing or Bush and Cheney causing 9/11.

There was no discernible reason for Trump to latch onto this idea; that is, beyond an inchoate dissatisfaction that caused him to doubt the authenticity of a black president. But when the target of his attack turned the tables on Trump, it is possible that the unexpected volley was enough to make him think the best revenge would be to tear down everything Obama had stood for.

Or the 2016 election could have turned out the way it did because ratings for Trump's reality show *Celebrity Apprentice* were down and he needed to find something else to do. Either way, America was due for a president like it had never seen before.

As the Obama presidency ended, there were widespread signs of dissatisfaction in both political parties. The Great Recession and its aftermath had inflicted further economic pain on a country that had already lost many jobs to globalization or automation. Neither party produced much in the way of remedies, especially for Americans without college degrees.

Republicans, beholden to business interests and thumbing through old Ayn Rand novels for inspiration, continued preaching about creating employment through lowering taxes and told nightmare parables about "job-killing" regulations. Democrats, enticed by the utopian promises of Silicon Valley, tossed out boilerplate about job retraining and mused about fantastic-sounding but ill-defined "green industry" jobs that were always just around the corner.

Democrats mobilized a massive grassroots network to elect Obama in 2008. But afterwards, that network was left untended. Complacency set in. Democrats remained unusually loyal, with over 90 percent approving of Obama's job performance by the end of 2016. Between the soaring heights of Obama's promises and the mundane reality of his governance—despite the ACA's expanding insurance coverage to 20 million Americans, his signature accomplishment looked incremental next to the society-changing legislation of Franklin Roosevelt or Lyndon Johnson—there was a gap filled by disappointment and a hunger for greater change than was endorsed by party leadership. An impatient cadre of Democrats had a laundry list of still-unresolved issues, particularly on immigration and labor. They would be hotly debated in the 2016 primary, more a contest of ideas than the party had seen in years.

The Republicans were undergoing their own internal strife. Just as the Democrats had failed to excite their core constituencies with middle-of-the-road candidates like Al Gore and John Kerry, the Republicans had been nominating men either too ideologically independent for the Fox News generation (John McCain) or too blandly corporate (Mitt Romney).

The country was becoming less socially conservative, less religious, and less white. These changes were not as dramatic as the non-Protestant immigrant surges of the late-nineteenth and early-twentieth centuries or even the social upheaval of the 1960s. But in response, already inspired by the brash religiosity and hooting anti-intel-lectualism of Sarah Palin, the Republican Party circled its wagons tighter around a native-born white, science-resistant Christian core. Between 2008 and 2016, the number of GOP presidential candidates admitting to a belief in evolution fell from three to one.[1]

There was every reason to think that 2016 would be a high-stakes election, but not particularly historic. Nota-ble presidents tend to be followed by dullards. But this election would prove to be the biggest party hijacking since the Democrats of 1896.

DONALD TRUMP

By the time Trump announced he was running in the 2016 election, he had been declared dead and resur-rected—usually in the pages of the New York tabloids he loved and courted so assiduously—more times than the average mortal. A character for whom the phrase "Only in America" might have been invented, he was a clown-haired bully and alleged con man wrapped in layers of obfuscation, lies, and puffery. A crashed real-estate mogul who roared back to fame playing a more successful version of himself on a reality TV show, he was a gadfly from Queens seeking approval from Man-hattan society; a social media addict who purveyed cheap branded goods and race-baiting conspiracy theo-ries; and a humorless P. T. Barnum whose main attrac-tion was himself.

Trump first started musing about running for president in the late 1980s, for roughly the same reasons as in 2016: his certainty that he would run the country better than anybody else, the notion that it might be good for his brand, and a vague curiosity about grabbing the brass ring. His first try was a brief pseudo-campaign for the Ross Perot–founded quasi-libertarian Reform Party. He came back to it in the early 2000s when his reality show *The Apprentice* was still going strong, and again in 2011, possibly as a way of stoking birtherism.

He officially announced his run for the Republican nomination in a June 2015 speech that praised China ("their leaders are much smarter"), preemptively touted his economic record ("I will be the greatest jobs president that God has ever created"), ogled his wealth ("I'm really rich"), and disparaged Mexican immigrants ("They're bringing drugs, they're bringing crime, they're rapists, and some, I assume, are good people").

This set the tone for everything that followed.

HILLARY CLINTON

By the time Hillary Clinton announced she was running in the 2016 election, she had been a national political figure for a quarter-century. She had also been the target of one of the most sophisticated, elongated, and punishing smear campaigns America has ever seen. A flinty combination of high careerism, deep policy knowledge, tactical reserve, and reality-battered idealism, she came of age at a time when women's contribution to politics was mostly restricted to uncredited work in the background, even in leftist circles. She learned the hard way how little trust much of the electorate had that a woman could lead the country as well as a man.

Raised in a comfortable Chicago suburb, Clinton received a law degree from Yale, where she met her future husband Bill Clinton. She went undercover to investigate whites-only "segregation academies" in Alabama for the Children's Defense Fund[2] and served on the presidential impeachment inquiry staff during Watergate. Through Bill's five terms as Arkansas governor, she bucked tradition and continued working, both teaching and practicing law.

During Bill's presidency, Hillary became the most visibly active First Lady in history, heading the national health care task force and advocating for women and children around the world. She also generated controversy, whipped up, as she famously said, by a "vast right-wing conspiracy." Her ambition, sharp humor, refusal to give up her career (a quip about not wanting to stay home and bake cookies was quickly characterized as an assault on stay-at-home mothers[3]), decision to stay with Bill after his affairs, and a reliably sexist media created a cartoon of her as power-mad tyrant (one magazine managed to compare her to Eva Peron, Lady Macbeth, *and* Winnie Mandela).[4] Though that image remained fixed for a segment of the population, she won election to the Senate from New York twice before being chosen by Obama as his Secretary of State in 2009.

When Clinton announced her run for the presidency in 2015, she had every reason to think she would be up against one of the many Republican governors and senators who overflowed the debate stage, most of whom she likely already knew. There was no reason for her to think she would have to worry about a nomination fight with a democratic socialist and end up competing against a real estate magnate who had never held public office.

THE ELECTION

The Democratic primary came down to a fight between Clinton and a raspy-voiced Brooklyn-born Vermont senator who tended to shout, wag his finger, and call for "revolution" to overthrow the "millionaires and billionaires" stealing the nation's wealth and leaving crumbs for working people. An unapologetic democratic socialist, Bernie Sanders upended every consultant and pundit's assumptions about what could play in American politics. Voicing many voters' raw economic discontent, he was the closest thing to a true populist outsider the party had seen in decades. Eventually Clinton recalibrated her positions enough to take some of Sanders' progressive support. Positioning herself as the more skilled and experienced choice, and emphasizing the historic possibility of being the first woman president, she pulled ahead.

A scrum of Republican candidates saw how close they could get to Tea Party talking points while still retaining non-party appeal for the general election. The presumptive nominee was George W. Bush's older brother Jeb.

Despite having been a popular governor of Florida and spending over $100 million, he was doomed by a lack of charisma, generic 1990s pro-business Republicanism, avoiding the culture-war trenches, and a moderate position on immigration. Running a shoestring campaign, Trump crashed around and soaked up airtime for saying outrageous things about immigrants, Muslims, political correctness, and his own "very good brain." Trump flouted the rules and beat up one rival after another.

By the time Trump and Clinton won their party nominations in July 2016, press coverage was feverishly high in a one-sided way, running Trump's rallies live and parsing each tweet while Clinton struggled to get reporters to care about what she said or did if it did not involve Trump. Some of the damage was self-inflicted, with an unclear message, defensive stance, and a campaign structure riddled with infighting.[5] But tactical errors aside, Clinton was also the first American presidential candidate to face not just a rival politician but domestic and foreign intelligence services.

Without birtherism to use, Trump had latched onto another conspiracy theory. In 2015, it was reported that Clinton had sometimes communicated through private rather than official government email, some of which was missing. Although Colin Powell had also used a private account while Secretary of State, "Hillary's emails" was seized on by Trump and right-wing media. An FBI investigation resulted in no charges but more bad press for Clinton in July 2016. Later that month, hacked emails from the Democratic National Committee were dumped on the Internet, causing even more bad press for the Clinton campaign. Days later, Trump called on Russia to find Clinton's missing emails. Russian government–directed hackers—already waging a sophisticated pro-Trump disinformation campaign to sow election chaos—targeted the Clinton campaign on or around the same day.[6]

Trump spent the rest of the campaign booming a "Make America Great Again" message right to the nostalgia, rage, and disaffection of a certain set of post–Tea Party voters. At raucous rallies, Trump stoked fear of immigrants and modernity, incited violence against protestors, and called the media "the enemy of the people." Unlike Clinton, with her carefully parsed incremental plans, he promised magical simplicity: better healthcare than Obamacare, the Washington "swamp" of corruption drained, factories sprouting across the land, a military so invincible the world would quail before it, prayer in schools, a security-swaddled America drowning in wealth. He repeatedly broke taboos so ingrained in American politics they had not even been articulated, from insulting John McCain's war record to calling for Clinton's arrest and refusing to apologize for statements that appeared to condone sexual assault (which Trump himself had been accused of by several women). He said the nation was broken and "I alone can fix it." Rally crowds, once tepid to McCain and Romney, roared the approval. While establishment Republican figures fretted, Trump stole their party.

Clinton was in a no-win situation. Being too circumspect resulted in negative coverage, but when she was unvarnished—saying at a fundraiser that half of Trump's supporters were a "basket of deplorables . . . racist, sexist, homophobic, xenophobic, Islamophobic"—that was more grist for the argument that Democrats were looking down their nose at Trump voters. In the fall of 2016, the Obama administration, concerned over being seen as interfering in an election, considered calling attention to how Russian military intelligence teams had hacked the Democratic Party and were pumping feverish anti-Clinton propaganda through social media. Assuming Clinton would win anyway and leave the government free to respond later, they held back.[7]

Even though the media narrative kept churning against her, Clinton ended up winning the popular election by roughly 3 million votes. But given the clustering of Democratic voters, not enough were in areas needed to carry the Electoral College. Overall voter turnout was on par with 2012, but relatively minor shifts in party enthusiasm (lower for Democrats, higher for Republicans) were enough to change the outcome.[8] In one of the biggest electoral jaw-droppers since Harry Truman pulled ahead of Thomas Dewey late in the night in 1948, Clinton's campaign came up roughly 78,000 votes short in Michigan, Pennsylvania, and Wisconsin.[9]

Given the choice between carrying on the principles of the Obama administration for another four years with a more experienced but less inspirational president and just blowing it all up, a significant minority of the electorate decided to pull the pin on an electoral grenade.

IT CAN HAPPEN HERE

—————

Worry quickly spread among non–Trump supporters that the country was under threat after the election of a race-baiting cult-of-personality president who emulated overseas dictators. Trying to mentally outfit themselves for a previously unimaginable future, many turned to fiction. Dystopian novels and TV adaptations that broadly echoed aspects of Trumpism, like *1984* (wrenching language and reality to fit authoritarian demands) and *The Handmaid's Tale* (subjugation of women), saw spikes in popularity, as did those specifically imagining fascist takeovers of America like *It Can Happen Here*, *The Man in the High Castle*, and *The Plot Against America*. Such imagined scenarios had long existed, but worries about fascism in the White House had generally been confined to the partisan fringes, where legitimate concerns about executive overreach sometimes bled into hyperbole. Post-2016, earnest discussion about the eroding of American democracy had entered the mainstream, making dystopian reading seem more relevant than ever.

THE AFTERMATH

The Founding Fathers were worried about a demagogue seizing power by leveraging the passions of a mob—what James Madison called "the mischiefs of faction." They intentionally dispersed powers through coequal branches of government and undercut the power of majority-rules voting with seemingly anti-democratic systems like the Electoral College and the Senate. But they had likely not imagined a scenario like 2016 and its aftermath, when the very institutions established to hold back a demagogue had been warped and infiltrated by a president's morally supine affiliates.

In 2016, President Trump wrenched the Republican Party off its moorings and reshaped it in his own image. In remarkably short order, the party that once championed free trade, muscular overseas interventions, fiscal conservatism, and moral probity had contorted itself away from all those positions and toward accommodating whatever the new president wanted.

Trump's task was made easier by the fact that Republicans had been tilting his way for some time. The torch of no-compromise conservatism lit by Palin in 2008, picked up by the Tea Party in 2009, and carried into Congress in 2010 was fueled by conspiracy theories that had shifted from the fringes to accepted discourse on Fox News and sincerely held beliefs of members of Congress.[10]

Habitual Republican Party discipline also helped the new commander in chief. Threatened with losing partisan media positions or elected offices, many of the "Never Trump" faction swiftly recalibrated their moral compasses and got back to work for the new boss. Those who did not were exiled and disparaged as "RINOs" (Republicans in Name Only). Tea Partiers who had railed about deficits and executive overreach under Obama now looked the other way.

Trump moved quickly to craft a signature agenda. In the first few months as president, he signed orders to build a Mexican border wall and to ban refugees and anyone from several majority-Muslim countries from entering America, pulled out of international trade and climate-change treaties, launched cruise missiles at Syria, and nominated a new Supreme Court justice. Echoing the neo-Confederate "bloody shirt" charges of the Reconstruction era, Trump and his allies dismissed criticism as "fake news" and railed about a supposed "deep state" conspiracy inside the government trying to sabotage his presidency. Unlike previous scandal-embroiled presidents, Trump sometimes announced his actions out in the open. During one interview, he proudly declared that he had fired the head of the FBI to stop an investigation of his campaign's alleged election coordination with Russia.

Trump governed as he campaigned: ignoring advice, reading nothing, going with his gut, keeping an eye on what would make good TV and benefit his family's company, and waging broad-spectrum asymmetric warfare on any person or institution that criticized him or pointed out inconvenient truths.

This permanent attack mode reflected a conflict resolution style he had employed since the federal government first sued him for housing discrimination in 1973.[11] At the same time, it reflected the party's radical turn. Not only had the GOP moved much further to the right than Democrats had moved to the left, but the ideological differences between mainstream and far-right Republicans had become more untenable.[12] The division was such that even though Republicans controlled the presidency and both houses of Congress after 2016, the only major legislation they were able to pass was a massive tax cut. Despite Trump's promises of boosting employment and not giving a handout to the wealthy, the bill overwhelmingly favored the rich and did little to help the economy.[13]

In a now-familiar pattern, the 2018 midterms became a referendum on the new administration. Infuriated by presidential tirades, staff chaos, the rise of white supremacist groups and related domestic terror attacks (including the 2018 massacre at a Pittsburgh synagogue carried out by a gunman whose anti-refugee beliefs echoed those of the president), a human-rights catastrophe at the Mexico border, befriending authoritarian regimes while criticizing allies, and general graft and incompetence, Democrats were energized.

A "Resistance" movement galvanized Democrats as the Tea Party had Republicans. After two years of marches, protests, and town halls denouncing Trump, a Democratic wave retook the House. Not long after, a seemingly unending parade of Democratic candidates began announcing for the 2020 election. Whether liberated or pushed to it by the party's newfound energy, many candidates advanced progressive policies that harkened back to Roosevelt and Johnson rather than the party's long chagrined post-Reagan era.

Democrats vacillated over whether to bother impeaching the president given that the Republican-held Senate would likely hold with historical precedent and vote to acquit. In September 2019, news broke that Trump had delayed military aid to Ukraine to pressure the country into investigating Democratic candidate Joe Biden. The simplicity of the accusation led to a sharp pivot toward impeachment.

By the time his impeachment inquiry ramped up in late 2019, Trump had failed to carry out many of his 2016 campaign promises: repeal and replace the ACA, build the border wall, bring back manufacturing jobs, "drain the swamp" of corruption, stop illegal immigration. Just as Herbert Hoover's Smoot-Hawley Tariff Act boomeranged negatively in 1930, Trump's scattershot trade wars with China and the European Union hurt rather than helped the domestic economy.[14]

Nevertheless, his support from the party faithful remained undiminished. On inauguration day, his job approval rating among Republicans was 89 percent. Nearly two years later it was 88 percent.[15] The only modern Republican president with higher average party approval was Ronald Reagan.[16]

The untethering of Trump's party approval from his performance indicated not only an unusually strong connection between a president and his supporters but also the likelihood that that support was based more on tenor and emotion than ideology. The same was likely true for Reagan; but his negative energies were primarily directed abroad. Most of Trump's antagonism was reserved for his fellow citizens, a target his followers approved of. Given that, and the degree to which Trump empowered the most aggrieved Republicans and enraged their Democratic opponents, the post-2016 era looked likely to be as factionalist as anything the country had seen since before the Civil War.

THE MUELLER INVESTIGATION

---◦◦◦◦◦---

The two-year special counsel investigation led by former FBI director Robert Mueller was assigned to look into Russian interference in the 2016 election. By the time he finished in March 2019, Mueller had established the scope and effect of that interference as well as how eagerly the Trump campaign had tried to obtain politically useful material from Russian entities. As a result of Mueller's investigation, dozens of Russians were indicted for stealing files from the Clinton campaign and Democratic National Committee and spreading pro-Trump propaganda through fake social media accounts. Several close Trump advisors were convicted on charges ranging from bank and tax fraud to hush-money payments to an adult film star. Concerned about what lay behind Trump's solicitous behavior toward Putin—rumors swirled about the president's financial obligations to shadowy oligarchs and banks with ties to the Kremlin—his opponents hoped Mueller's investigation would present evidence of collusion with a foreign power. But Watergate-era legal precedent held that a sitting president could not be criminally charged. Mueller was also circumspect about his role's limitations. The report's dismal catalogue of cover-ups and venality, while rife with potentially impeachable content, did not include a criminal referral or black-and-white evidence of close coordination between the Trump campaign and the Russian disinformation campaign.

WHAT IF...?

Many factors favored Trump in 2016, from media obsession over the email controversy to Democratic tactical errors. His unlikely victory was described as "the political equivalent of getting dealt a Royal Flush in poker."[17] Given that, it is easy to imagine things going the other way. If Clinton had held only a slightly larger percentage of Obama's support from 2012, she would have become the forty-fifth president and first woman to lead the nation.

A Clinton presidency would have been historic, with First Man Bill Clinton taking a back seat as his wife exercised her duties as leader of the free world. It also would have been a battle, as a slim victory may have left Congress in Republican hands. Days before the 2016 election, several House Republican committee chairmen declared they would investigate and potentially impeach Clinton immediately after she took office.[18] The email controversy would not have abated, nor would claims of foreign corruption deriving from Bill's international fundraising for the Clinton Foundation. (Without feeling a need to defend the Trump family's pursuit of foreign business deals while he was president, Republicans would have likely been even more aggressive investigating Clinton.)

Clinton's loyalty to Obama in 2016 stopped her from advocating anything that could be misconstrued as a break in the ranks, even when it might have helped her.[19] Nevertheless, her campaign proposals were far more progressive than her centrist 2008 platform: eliminating in-state college tuition for most students, a quarter-trillion-dollar infrastructure program, comprehensive immigration reform, and increasing the federal minimum wage.[20] She planned to build on the ACA by allowing people to buy in to a government insurance program, the so-called "public option." This idea was deemed too radical for Obama to pursue in 2008, but by 2020 it had nearly become a baseline Democratic belief.

Given Clinton's global expertise and relationships built during her years as Secretary of State, there is a good chance she would have focused on foreign affairs. Indications are that Clinton's foreign policy would have been somewhat more interventionist and less cautious than Obama's but still prudent enough to avoid the overextension of the Bush years. Many foreign-policy missteps of the Trump years may have been avoided, including squabbles with NATO, pulling out of the Iran nuclear deal without a viable backup plan, and withdrawing troops from the fight against ISIS in Syria without warning. Her most crucial foreign-policy challenge would have been Russia. Due to Putin's long animus toward Clinton, her human-rights and democracy advocacy would likely have been viewed as a threat to his power, almost certainly resulting in the continuation of Russia's disinformation warfare if it had failed to elect a more pliable candidate like Trump.

In 2020, Clinton would have faced an uphill fight. Since Roosevelt and Truman, no party had held the presidency for more than three consecutive terms. Conservatives would have been eager for a showdown after four years of watching Trump and his fellow travelers bemoan the unfairness of their loss.

Given Democrats' complacency during the Obama presidency, it is difficult to imagine a large enough turn-out to ensure Clinton's reelection. Clinton's best chance for a second term probably would have been a subpar Republican candidate, a not-unlikely possibility given that the party's more ideologically pure stars often came with significant baggage, questionable beliefs, or low-wattage stage appeal.

Without a President Trump, the post-2016 American political scene would have been chaotic and divisive but ultimately far more recognizable to those of previous generations.

What remains to be seen is whether the presidents who follow Trump carry out their duties as though he were an aberration in a centuries-long democratic tradition or a new norm.

—————◦◦◦◦◦◦—————

ENDNOTES

1796
JOHN ADAMS vs. THOMAS JEFFERSON

1 Banner, James M. editor. *Presidential Misconduct* (New York: The New Press, 2019), xxvi.

2 Chernow, Ron. *Washington: A Life* (New York: Penguin Books, 2010), 568.

3 Smith, Page. "Election of 1796," *History of American Presidential Elections, 1789–2001, Vol. 1* (Philadelphia: Chelsea House, 2002), 59.

4 *The Portable John Adams* (New York: Penguin, 2004), 236.

5 Mieczkowski, Yanek. *The Routledge Historical Atlas of Presidential Elections* (New York: Routledge, 2001), 18.

6 Library of Congress. http://bit.ly/2TEP4JG. Accessed August 17, 2019.

7 Chernow, Ron. *Alexander Hamilton* (New York: Penguin Press, 2004), 571.

8 Ellis, Joseph. *His Excellency George Washington* (New York: Knopf, 2004), 245.

1828
ANDREW JACKSON vs. JOHN QUINCY ADAMS

1 CQ Press. *Presidential Elections 1789–2000* (Washington, D.C.: CQ Press, 2002), 24.

2 Traub, James. *John Quincy Adams: Militant Spirit* (New York: Basic Books, 2016), 318.

3   Remini, Robert. "Andrew Jackson and His Indian Wars."
    New York Times, July 15, 2001.

4   Meacham, Jon. *American Lion: Andrew Jackson in the White
    House* (New York: Random House, 2008), 29.

5   Tocqueville, Alexis de. *Democracy in America* (New York:
    Barnes & Noble Publishing, 2003), 154.

6   Heidler, David S., and Jeanne T. Heidler. *The Rise of
    Andrew Jackson: Myth, Manipulation, and the Making of
    Modern Politics* (New York: Hachette, 2018).

7   "The Tsunami of Slime Circa 1828." *New York*, June 15,
    2012.

8   Remini, Robert. *Henry Clay: Statesman for the Union*
    (New York: W. W. Norton, 1991), 325.

9   Thomas, Louisa. "Watching Andrew Jackson's Inauguration."
    New Yorker, January 19, 2017. https://www.newyorker.com/
    news/news-desk/watching-andrew-jacksons-inauguration.
    Accessed August 27, 2019.

10 United States Election Project. http://www.electproject.org/
    national-1789-present. Accessed August 27, 2019.

11 Meacham, 61.

12 Inskeep, Steve. "How Jackson Made a Killing in Real
    Estate." *Politico*, July 4, 2015.

13 Remini, Robert V. *Andrew Jackson: The Course of American
    Freedom: 1822–1832* (Baltimore: Johns Hopkins University
    Press, 1981), 291.

14 Howe, Daniel Walker. *What Hath God Wrought:
    The Transformation of America, 1815–1848* (New York:
    Oxford University Press, 2007), 494.

15 Meacham, 299.

1860
ABRAHAM LINCOLN vs. STEPHEN DOUGLAS

1 Shafer, Ronald. *Carnival Campaign* (Chicago: Chicago Review Press, 2016).

2 O'Brien, Cormac. *Secret Lives of the U.S. Presidents* (Philadelphia: Quirk Books, 2004), 79.

3 Freeman, Joanne B. *The Field of Blood: Violence in Congress and the Road to the Civil War* (New York: Farrar, Straus and Giroux, 2018).

4 C-SPAN. "Presidential Historians Survey 2017." https://www.c-span.org/presidentsurvey2017/?page=overall. Accessed August 31, 2019.

5 Matuz, Roger. *The Presidents Fact Book* (New York: Black Dog & Leventhal, 2017), 254.

6 Goodwin, Doris Kearns. *Team of Rivals: The Political Genius of Abraham Lincoln* (New York: Simon & Schuster, 2005), 204.

7 Hindley, Meredith. "The Man Who Came in Second," *Humanities*. November/December 2010.

8 McPherson, James. "What Did He Really Think About Race?" *New York Review of Books*, March 29, 2007.

9 McPherson, James. *Battle Cry of Freedom* (New York: Oxford University Press, 1988), 212.

10 Meacham, 355.

11 Goodwin, 346.

12 Jenkins, Mark Collins. "Civil War at 150: How a Bloodless Battle Started It All." *National Geographic*, April 13, 2001.

13 Holzer, Harold. "Election Day 1860." *Smithsonian*, November 2008.

1876
RUTHERFORD B. HAYES vs. SAMUEL J. TILDEN

1 Masur, Louis P. *Lincoln's Last Speech: Wartime Reconstruction and the Crisis of Reunion* (New York: Oxford University Press, 2015), xiv.

2 Bordewich, Fergus. "The Election That Saved the United States." *Wall Street Journal*, August 29, 2014.

3 "Reconstruction vs. Redemption." *Humanities*, February 11, 2014.

4 White, Ronald C. *American Ulysses: A Life of Ulysses S. Grant* (New York: Random House, 2016), 551.

5 ———. "Ulysses S. Grant." *The Presidents*, eds. Brian Lamb, Susan Swain, C-SPAN (New York: Public Affairs, 2019), 266.

6 Loewen, James. "Five myths about why the South seceded." *Washington Post*, February 26, 2011.

7 Hoogenboom, Ari. "Rutherford B. Hayes." *The Presidents*, eds. Brian Lamb, Susan Swain, C-SPAN (New York: Public Affairs, 2019), 366.

8 Morris Jr., Roy. *Fraud of the Century: Rutherford B. Hayes, Samuel Tilden, and the Stolen Election of 1876* (New York: Simon & Schuster, 2003), 15.

9 Boller Jr., Paul F. *Presidential Campaigns* (New York: Oxford University Press, 1984), 134.

10 Bellesiles, Michael A. *1877: America's Year of Living Violently* (New York: The New Press, 2010), 44.

11 Gates, Henry Louis. *Stony the Road: Reconstruction, White Supremacy, and the Rise of Jim Crow* (New York: Penguin Press, 2019), 31–35, 187.

12 Budiansky, Stephen. *The Bloody Shirt: Terror After Appomattox* (New York: Viking, 2008), 4.

1896
WILLIAM MCKINLEY vs. WILLIAM JENNINGS BRYAN

1   Matuz, Roger. *The Presidents Fact Book* (New York: Black Dog & Leventhal, 2017), 356.

2   Ciccone, F. Richard. "The Power of Myth," *Chicago Tribune*, August 26, 1996.

3   Green, Donald J. *Third-Party Matters: Politics, Presidents, and Third Parties in American History* (Santa Barbara, CA: Praeger, 2010), 36.

4   Lepore, Jill. "Blatherskites," *New Yorker*, May 16, 2011.

5   Leech, Margaret. "The Front Porch Campaign," *American Heritage*, December 1959.

6   Library of Congress, "Songs of Politics and Political Campaigns." https://www.loc.gov/collections/songs-of -america/articles-and-essays/historical-topics/songs-of -politics-and-political-campaigns/. Accessed September 8, 2019.

7   Kazin, Michael. "The Forgotten Forerunner," *Wilson Quarterly*, Autumn 1999.

8   Phillips, Kevin. *William McKinley* (New York: Times Books, 2003), 34.

9   Leech.

10 Beschloss, Michael. *Presidents of War* (New York: Crown, 2018), 259.

11 Kinzer, Stephen. *The True Flag: Theodore Roosevelt, Mark Twain, and the Birth of the American Empire* (New York: Henry Holt, 2017), 94.

12 Richman, Michael. "'A Splendid Little War' Built America's Empire," *Washington Post*, April 8, 1998.

1932
FRANKLIN DELANO ROOSEVELT vs. HERBERT HOOVER

1   Thomas, Heather. "The Pocket Items That Saved the Life of Theodore Roosevelt," Library of Congress, July 30, 2019.

2   Smith, Richard Norton and Timothy Walch. "The Ordeal of Herbert Hoover, Part 2," *Prologue*, Summer 2006.

3   Coates, Ta-Nehisi. "The Case for Reparations," *The Atlantic*, June 2014.

4   Daniels, Roger. *Franklin D. Roosevelt: Road to the New Deal, 1882–1939* (Champaign, IL: University of Illinois Press, 2015), 13.

5   Smith, Richard Norton and Timothy Walch. "The Ordeal of Herbert Hoover," *Prologue*, Summer 2004.

6   "The Worst Convention in U.S. History?" *Politico Magazine*, July 22, 2016.

7   Boller, Paul F. *Presidential Campaigns: From George Washington to George W. Bush* (New York: Oxford University Press, 2004), 234.

8   Franklin D. Roosevelt Presidential Library and Museum. http://www.fdrlibrary.marist.edu/_resources/images/msf/ msf00534. Accessed September 22, 2019.

9   Boller, 236.

10 Dickson, Paul and Thomas B. Allen. "Marching on History," *Smithsonian*, February 2003.

11 Alter, Jonathan. *The Defining Moment: FDR's Hundred Days and the Triumph of Hope* (New York: Simon & Schuster, 2006), 5.

12 Phillips-Fein, Kim. "Fear and Loathing of the Green New Deal," *New Republic*, May 29, 2019.

13 "Gen. Butler Bares 'Fascist Plot' to Seize Government by Force," *New York Times*, November 21, 1934.

14 "Wilkie objects," *LIFE*, September 16, 1940.

15 Leuchtenburg, William Edward. *The FDR Years: On Roosevelt and His Legacy* (New York: Columbia University Press, 1995), 5.

16 Black, Eric. "Walter Mondale defends torture report, rejects CIA response," *MinnPost*, December 22, 2014.

17 Denton, Sally. *The Plots Against the President: FDR, a Nation in Crisis, and the Rise of the American Right* (New York: Bloomsbury, 2012), 52.

18 Benzkofer, Stephan, "Tell Chicago I'll Pull Through," *Chicago Tribune*, February 10, 2013.

1964
LYNDON B. JOHNSON vs. BARRY GOLDWATER

1 Muntaglio, Bill, and Steven L. Davis. *Dallas 1963* (New York: Hachette, 2013).

2 Graff, Garrett M. "Angel is Airborne." *Washingtonian*, November 2013.

3 Beschloss, Michael. "Lyndon Johnson on the Record." *Texas Monthly*, December 2001.

4 Caro, Robert A. *The Years of Lyndon Johnson: The Passage of Power* (New York: Vintage, 2012) 3.

5 Goldwater, Barry. *The Conscience of a Conservative* (Victor Publishing, Shepherdsville, KY), 13.

6   Smith, Richard Norton. *On His Own Terms: A Life of Nelson Rockefeller* (New York: Random House, 2014) xix.

7   Alsop, Stewart. "Can Goldwater Win in 64?" *The Saturday Evening Post*, August 24, 1963.

8   Goldwater, 34.

9   Flamm, Michael W. *Law and Order: Street Crime, Civil Unrest, and the Crisis of Liberalism in the 1960s.* New York: Columbia University Press, 2005.

10   Rockefeller, Nelson. "Remarks on Extremism at the 1964 Republican National Convention." Rockefeller Archive Center.

11   Zirin, Dave. "Ken Burns on Jackie Robinson and the Republican Party's 'Pact with the Devil'." *The Nation*, April 11, 2016.

12   Gerson, Michael. "Barry Goldwater's Warning to the GOP." *Washington Post.* April 17, 2014.

13   Perlstein, Rick. *Before the Storm: Barry Goldwater and the Unmaking of the American Consensus* (Hachette: New York, 2001) 310.

14   "The Tonkin Gulf." The Miller Center, University of Virginia. http://bit.ly/2Zxnm3s. Accessed August 4, 2019.

15   Boroson, Warren. "What Psychiatrists Say About Goldwater." *Fact*, September–October 1964.

16   Nichols, David A. "Ike Liked Civil Rights." *New York Times*, September 12, 2007.

17   Weeks, Edward. "The 1964 Election." *The Atlantic*, October 1964.

18   CQ Press. *Presidential Elections 1789–2000* (Washington, D.C.: CQ Press, 2002), 69.

19 Menand, Louis. "He Knew He Was Right," *New Yorker*, March 18, 2001.

20 *New York Times*. "Goldwater: 'If Elected, I'll Ask' Eisenhower to Go to Vietnam." October 6, 1964.

1980
RONALD REAGAN vs. JIMMY CARTER

1 Jacobs, Ron. *The Way the Wind Blew: A History of the Weather Underground* (New York: Verso, 1997), 157.

2 Perlstein, Rick. *The Invisible Bridge: The Fall of Nixon and the Rise of Reagan* (New York: Simon & Schuster, 2014), 802.

3 Reagan, Ronald. *An American Life* (New York: Simon & Schuster, 1990), 21.

4 Kopelson, Gene. "'The Speech': When Reagan Electrified America, and Transformed It," *National Review*, April 30, 2016.

5 Matuz, Roger. *The Presidents Fact Book* (New York: Black Dog & Leventhal, 2017), 658.

6 Frank, Jeffrey. "The Primary Experiment: Jimmy Who?" *New Yorker*, May 1, 2015.

7 Kilgore, Ed. "How Jimmy Carter's Election Previewed Trump's," *New York*, March 23, 2019.

8 Fallows, James. "The Passionless Presidency," *The Atlantic*, May 1979.

9 "Whip His What?" *Time*, June 25, 1979.

10 Ward, Jon. "The Humiliating Handshake and the Near-Fistfight that Broke the Democratic Party," *Politico Magazine*, January 21, 2019.

11   "Public Trust in Government: 1958–2019," Pew Research
      Center, April 11, 2019.

12   Stein, Ellin. "The President Who Wanted Us to Stop
      Climate Change," *Slate*, September 21, 2019.

13   Bartlett, Bruce. "Reagan's Forgotten Tax Record," *Tax
      Notes*, Vol. 130, No. 8, 2011.

14   Congressional Quarterly, *Budgeting for America*, 1982,
      p. 99.

15   Weisberg, Jacob. *Ronald Reagan* (New York: Times Books,
      2016), 70.

16   Wittner, Lawrence. "Eliminating the Danger," *Boston
      Review*, April 1, 2000.

17   Ubel, Peter. "The Biggest Government Health Care
      Spender Since LBJ Was…Ronald Reagan?" *Forbes*,
      February 28, 2014.

18   Kornacki, Steve. "The New Teflon President," *Observer*,
      June 19, 2009.

19   "Landslide Victory by Reagan Underscores Democratic Ills,"
      CQ Almanac 1984.

20   Suri, Jeremi. *Presidential Misconduct*. Edited by James M.
      Banner (New York: The New Press, 2019), 405

2008
BARACK OBAMA vs. JOHN MCCAIN

1   Mieczkowski, Yanek. *The Routledge Historical Atlas of
     Presidential Elections* (New York: Routledge, 2001), 143.

2   Thomson, Hunter S. *Kingdom of Fear: Loathsome Secrets
     of a Star-Crossed Child in the Final Days of the American
     Century* (New York: Simon & Schuster, 2003), 165.

3   Remnick, David. *The Bridge: The Life and Rise of Barack Obama* (New York: Alfred A. Knopf, 2010), 405.

4   Gooding, Richard. "The Trashing of John McCain," *Vanity Fair*, September 24, 2008.

5   Martin, Jonathan and Amie Parnes. "McCain: Obama not an Arab, crowd boos," *Politico*, October 10, 2008.

6   Blumenthal, Max. *Republican Gomorrah: Inside the Movement that Shattered the Party* (New York: Nation Books, 2009), 11.

7   Bump, Philip. "Sarah Palin cost John McCain 2 million votes in 2008, according to a study," *Washington Post*, January 19, 2016.

8   Alter, Jonathan. *The Promise: President Obama, Year One* (New York: Simon & Schuster, 2010), 245.

9   Garrow, David. "Barack Obama," *The Presidents*, eds. Brian Lamb, Susan Swain, C-SPAN (New York: Public Affairs, 2019), 159.

10   Bishop, Bill. *The Big Sort: Why the Clustering of Like-Minded Americans is Tearing Us Apart* (New York: Houghton Mifflin, 2008), 10.

11   Alberta, Tim. *American Carnage: On the Front Lines of the Republican Civil War and the Rise of President Trump* (New York: Harper, 2019), 41.

12   Nesbit, Jeff. "The Secret Origins of the Tea Party," *Time*, April 5, 2016.

13   Frank, Thomas. *Pity the Billionaire: The Hard-Times Swindle and the Unlikely Comeback of the Right* (New York: Metropolitan Books, 2012), 43.

14   DeSilver, Drew. "U.S. income inequality, on rise for decades, is now highest since 1928," Pew Research Center, December 5, 2013.

15 Younis, Mohamed. "Most Blacks Rate Race Relations With Whites as Bad," *Gallup*, February 21, 2019.

16 Southern Poverty Law Center, "Hate groups reach record high," February 19, 2019.

17 Rothkopf, David. "Obama's 'Don't Do Stupid Shit' Foreign Policy," *Foreign Policy*, June 4, 2014.

2016
DONALD TRUMP vs. HILLARY CLINTON

1 Andersen, Kurt. *Fantasyland: How America Went Haywire, A 500-Year History* (New York: Random House, 2017), 372.

2 Rodham Clinton, Hillary. *Living History* (New York: Scribner, 2003), 57.

3 White, Daniel. "A Brief History of the Clinton Family's Chocolate-Chip Cookies," *Time*, August 19, 2016.

4 Wattenberg, Daniel. "The Lady Macbeth of Little Rock," *American Spectator*, August 1992.

5 Allen, Jonathan and Amie Parnes. *Shattered: Inside Hillary Clinton's Doomed Campaign* (New York: Crown, 2017), x.

6 Hendry, Erica R. "Trump asked Russia to find Clinton's emails. On or around the same day, Russians targeted her accounts," *PBS NewsHour*, July 13, 2018.

7 Osnos, Evan, David Remnick and Joshua Yaffa. "Trump, Putin, and the New Cold War," *New Yorker*, March 6, 2017.

8 Center for American Progress. "Voter Trends in 2016: A Final Examination," November 1, 2017.

9 Cook, Charlie. "The Odds of a 2016 Redux," *The Cook Political Report*, July 26, 2019.

10   Alberta, Tim. *American Carnage: On the Front Lines of the Republican Civil War and the Rise of President Trump* (New York: Harper, 2019), 94.

11   Kaplan, Morris. "Major Landlord Accused of Antiblack Bias in City," *New York Times*, October 16, 1973.

12   Faris, David. "Why the GOP Congress will be the most unproductive in 164 years," *The Week*. July 18, 2017.

13   Steverman, Ben, Dave Merrill and Jeremy C.F. Lin. "A Year After the Middle Class Tax Cut, the Rich are Winning," *Bloomberg*, December 18, 2018.

14   Swanson, Ana. "Trump's Trade War Could Put Swiss-Size Dent in Global Economy, I.M.F. Warns," October 8, 2019.

15   "Presidential Approval Ratings – Donald Trump," Gallup, https://news.gallup.com/poll/203198/presidential-approval -ratings-donald-trump.aspx. Accessed October 12, 2019.

16   "Presidential Job Approval Center," Gallup, https://news. gallup.com/interactives/185273/presidential-job-approval -center.aspx. Accessed October 12, 2019.

17   Bitecofer, Rachel. "With 16 Months to go, Negative Partisanship Predicts the 2020 Presidential Election," Judy Ford Wason Center for Public Policy, July 1, 2019. http://cnu.edu/wasoncenter/2019/07/01-2020-election -forecast/. Accessed October 20, 2019.

18   DeBonis, Mike. "Some Republicans are discussing their plans for President Clinton – starting with impeachment," *Washington Post*, November 3, 2016.

19   Greenberg, Stanley. "How She Lost," *The American Prospect*, September 21, 2017

20   "Hillary's Vision for America," https://www.hillaryclinton. com/issues/. Accessed October 13, 2019.

TIMELINE OF VOTING RIGHTS

1788-1789

For the first presidential election, individual states are given the power to determine voting eligibility. Only white, male landowners or taxpayers could vote (6 percent of the population).

1828

Religious restrictions on voting rights are officially removed in every state when Maryland grants Jewish citizens the right to vote.

1848

The first women's rights convention is held in Seneca Falls, New York, where attendees pass a resolution demanding suffrage for women.

1856

All white males, regardless of property ownership, become eligible to vote.

1868

The 14th amendment grants citizenship rights to African-American men, but stops short of suffrage.

1870

The 15th amendment prohibits the government from denying any male citizens the right to vote on the basis of "race, color, or previous condition of servitude."

1872

Women's rights activist Susan B. Anthony casts a ballot in the presidential election and is arrested two weeks later. Abolitionist and women's rights activist Sojourner Truth also attempts to vote in Michigan, but is denied.

1884

The Supreme Court decision in *Elk v. Wilkins* denies Native Americans eligibility for citizenship and, consequently, the right to vote.

1920

All American women are granted the right to vote upon ratification of the 19th amendment.

1924

Native Americans are granted citizenship by the Indian Citizenship Act, but not guaranteed voting rights in all states until 1962.

1961

The 23rd amendment gives the residents of Washington, D.C., the right to vote in presidential elections, but not representation in Congress.

1964

The 24th amendment prohibits state and federal governments from requiring payment of a poll tax in order to vote.

1965

President Johnson signs the Voting Rights Act, which outlaws practices that deny citizens their right to vote based on racial discrimination.

1971

The 26th amendment allows all citizens aged 18 years and older the right to vote.

1975

Amendments to the Voting Rights Act prohibit literacy tests and require voting materials be printed in languages other than English, so non-English-speaking citizens could vote.

1990

President George H. W. Bush signs into law the Americans with Disabilities Act, which ensures accessibility to all aspects of the voting process for citizens with disabilities.

1993

The National Voter Registration Act eases the registration process by permitting mail-in registration and requiring DMVs, public-assistance offices, and various state-funded agencies to offer registration opportunities for all citizens.

2002

After the controversial 2000 election results that saw the rejection of nearly 2 million ballots due to flaws in the punch-card and lever system, President George W. Bush signs the Help America Vote Act, which creates the Election Assistance Commission and initiates sweeping reforms to upgrade voting machines and election procedures.

2009

President Obama signs the Military and Overseas Empowerment Act, which facilitates the voting process for members of the military and citizens residing abroad primarily through online delivery and tracking systems.

MAJOR POLITICAL PARTIES

Federalist (1791–1824)

The only American political party whose origin can be traced to a collection of essays, the Federalists took their inspiration from Alexander Hamilton, John Jay, and James Madison's *Federalist Papers*. Despite many of the Founding Fathers' antipathy toward parties, the Federalists formed very early in the republic's history and helped shape a good part of its formation at a malleable time. Essentially a Hamiltonian faction, the party supported a powerful central government and institutions rather than a dispersal of authority amongst the states. At a time when tensions between America, Britain, and France remained high, the Federalists were seen as the pro-British faction. Although they could only claim one president, John Adams (1796), as the first chief executive elected after George Washington, he played an outsize role in the early delineation of the office's traditions and powers. After Adams, the party's lack of electioneering skill and general disunity resulted in its relatively quick disintegration. Their legacy lived on somewhat in the Republican Party.

Democratic (1792–present)

Formed by disgruntled anti-Federalists who liked nothing about the towering edifices of centralized federal power that the Hamiltonians were erecting in the late eighteenth century, the Democratic-Republicans were originally an opposition faction who followed their leader Thomas Jefferson's support of decentralization and states' rights. Later they adopted more emphatically populist notions (which overlapped with their distrust of the Federalists, seen as more urban and elitist) under the leadership of Andrew Jackson. A fractious lot, they first split in 1825 between the Jacksonian Democratic wing and the National Republicans, who soon became the Whig Party. They renamed themselves the Democratic Party in 1844, after debates over slavery caused a schism and the creation of the offshoot Republicans.

Following the Civil War, the Democrats created a lock on Southern state legislatures that lasted well into the mid-twentieth century. During that time, Democrats comprised a somewhat schizophrenic organization, representing more traditionalist reactionary and racist elements in the South and more liberal-leaning urban dwellers and immigrants in the North. Once the nation fell into its bipartisan groove, the Democrats were generally seen as both the more populist and federalist of the two, with presidents like Franklin Delano Roosevelt and Lyndon Baines Johnson leveraging federal authority on behalf of the poor, working class, and minorities.

The country's oldest political party, the Democrats are today identified as America's mainstream liberal party, somewhat analogous to but more conservative than European social democratic parties.

Whig (1834–54)

A somewhat short-lived second-string party that never-theless played a notable role in mid-nineteenth-century politics, the Whigs were a starchy band of anti-Jackso-nians (once known as the National Republicans) who took their inspiration from the British anti-royalist party of the same name. Unable to coalesce around anything more cohesive than Jacksonian Democrat opposition and supporting national infrastructure and the Bank of the United States, the Whigs fell apart in the 1850s after fail-ing to present a united position on slavery. Many of the northern Whigs then absconded for the Republican Party. Some others splintered off into the Know-Nothing Party, a xenophobic band of nineteenth-century deplorables.

Although in their mere two decades of existence, the Whigs sent two presidents to the White House—William Henry Harrison (1840) and Zachary Taylor (1848)—that impressive statistic is colored by the fact that both died in office. They were replaced respectively by vice presidents John Tyler (who, once in office, turned staunchly anti-Whig) and the remarkably unremarkable Millard Fillmore.

Republican (1854–present)

Laid bare by the slavery debates of the 1840s and '50s, divisions in the Democratic Party became so acrimoni-ous that in 1854 a splinter faction, which also included some Whigs and abolitionist Free-Soilers, was estab-lished. Calling themselves the Republican Party, they ascended to the White House in 1860 with Abraham Lincoln, their first (and by many accounts greatest) president. After establishing their bona fides as the party that freed the slaves and kept the Union together, the Republicans became the other half of the bipartisan system that (but for interruptions by short-lived insurgent parties like the Populists) comprised American politics for the next century and a half.

Republican protectionism and a more conservative stance toward governance gained them the support of the business community. By the time of FDR's New Deal, the Republicans were fully aligned with monied, establishment interests. In the years after World War II, the "Party of Lincoln" began to adopt a more populist conservative and racially reactionary viewpoint that put it at loggerheads with a Democratic Party that was becoming more socially liberal. In the present day, Republicans are the country's mainstream conservative party, with a more nationalistic fervor than is seen in their European counterparts like Britain's Tories.

FURTHER READING

Adams, John. *The Portable John Adams*. New York: Penguin, 2004.

Alberta, Tim. *American Carnage: On the Front Lines of the Republican Civil War and the Rise of President Trump*. New York: Harper, 2019.

Alter, Jonathan. *The Promise: President Obama, Year One*. New York: Simon & Schuster, 2010.

Banner, James M. *Presidential Misconduct*. New York: The New Press, 2019.

Beschloss, Michael. *Presidents of War*. New York: Crown, 2018.

Boller, Paul F., Jr. *Presidential Campaigns*. New York: Oxford University Press, 2004.

Caro, Robert. *The Passage of Power: The Years of Lyndon Johnson, Vol. 4*. New York: Vintage, 2012.

Chernow, Ron. *Alexander Hamilton*. New York: Penguin Press, 2004.

Chernow, Ron. *Washington: A Life*. New York: Penguin Books, 2010.

de Tocqueville, Alexis. *Democracy in America*. New York: Library of America, 2004.

Ellis, Joseph. *His Excellency George Washington*. New York: Knopf, 2004.

Gates, Henry Louis, Jr. *Stony the Road: Reconstruction, White Supremacy, and the Rise of Jim Crow*. New York: Penguin Press, 2019.

Goodwin, Doris Kearns. *Team of Rivals: The Political Genius of Abraham Lincoln*. New York: Simon & Schuster, 2005.

Hamilton, Alexander, John Jay, James Madison. *The Federalist Papers*. New York: J. & A. McLean, 1788.

Meacham, Jon. *American Lion: Andrew Jackson in the White House*. New York: Random House, 2008.

Morris, Edmund. *Dutch: A Memoir of Ronald Reagan*. New York: Random House, 1999.

Perlstein, Rick. *The Invisible Bridge: The Fall of Nixon and the Rise of Reagan*. New York: Simon & Schuster, 2014.

Schlesinger, Arthur M., Jr. *The Imperial Presidency*. New York: Mariner Books, 1973.

ABOUT THE AUTHOR

Chris Barsanti is the author of several books. His writing has been published in the *Chicago Tribune*, the *Virginia Quarterly Review*, the *Barnes & Noble Review*, *Publishers Weekly*, *Rain Taxi Review of Books*, and the *Minneapolis Star-Tribune*. No matter how old he gets, he always displays the "I Voted" sticker on Election Day.